UNIVERSITY MEETS MICROFINANCE AWARDS

University Meets Microfinance (UMM) presents its eleventh "UMM Award":

In order to foster and promote new research on topics related to financial inclusion and recognize the work of young researchers, UMM rewards and publishes outstanding student research each year. The UMM Award winners are selected by a Selection Committee composed of qualified academics and practitioners working in the financial inclusion domain.

Daniela Röttger received a Master of Arts in International Relations and Development Policy from the University of Duisburg – Essen in October 2013 and received the 2013 UMM award for her thesis titled "Agricultural Finance for Smallholder Farmers: Rethinking Traditional Microfinance Risk and Cost Management Approaches".

Special thanks to the following Selection Committee members for their valuable time and participation in the 2013 UMM Awards selection process:

Academics: Bernd Balkenhol (Université de Genève); Christina May (Universität Köln); Fernando Rodriguez (Universidad de Salamanca); Friederike Lenel (DIW); Klaas Molenaar and Julie-Marthe Lehmann (The Hague University of Applied Sciences); Kristina Czura (CERDI - Université d'Auvergne); Pauline Bensoussan (Sciences Po); Robert Lensink (Universität Groningen); Roberto Moro Visconti (Università Cattolica del Sacro Cuore Milano); Sergio Bortolani (Università Degli Studi Di Torino); Thea Nielsen (Universität Hohenheim); Thilo Klein (University of Cambridge); Yasmin Olteanu (Freie Universität Berlin)

Practitioners: Anaar Kara, Karla Henning and Sébastien Weber (PlaNet Guarantee); Andrea Limone (PerMicro); Daniela Pensotti, Delphine Bazalgette, Francisco Escamilla, Maud Chalamet, Simon Priollaud and Vanessa Quintero (PlaNet Finance); Diego Luigi Dagradi and Maria Cristina Negro (Fondazione Giordano Dell'Amore); Hansjorg Kessler (FIDES); Kathleen Welvers (GIZ); Oliver Gloede (European Central Bank); Philippe Guichandut (Grameen Crédit Agricole); Verónica López Sabater (Fundación AFI)

This publication has been made possible thanks to the financial support of:

This book has been produced with the financial assistance of the European Union.
The content of this publication are the sole responsibility of PlaNet Finance and can under no circumstances be regarded as reflecting the position of the European Union.

ABOUT UNIVERSITY MEETS MICROFINANCE

edited by PlaNet Finance Deutschland e.V.

ISSN 2190-2291

The growing interest of students and academics as well as the increasing need for knowledge creation and dissemination in the microfinance sector, led to the launch of University Meets Microfinance (UMM) by PlaNet Finance and Freie Universität Berlin in 2009.

UMM is a European initiative which fosters cooperation between European universities, students and microfinance practitioners to promote microfinance and financial inclusion education and innovation through research. UMM is active in the domains of microfinance education, research, documentation of information, professional exchange & dissemination of information. All UMM activities are carried out under the umbrella of the European Microfinance Platform (e-MFP) in the frame of the e-MFP UMM Action Group.

From 2009 to 2013, more than 4.600 students, academics and practitioners have benefitted from UMM activities.

CONTACT AND FOLLOW UMM:

www.universitymeetsmicrofinance.eu
www.e-mfp.eu/action-groups/university-meets-microfinance
umm@planetfinance.org
www.facebook.com/universitymeetsmicrofinance

Volumes

9   Thilo Klein
    Why Do India's Urban Poor Choose to Go Private?
    Health Policy Simulations in Slums of Hyderabad
    ISBN 978-3-8382-0238-9

10 Nicole Tode
    Transforming Microfinance Institutions
    A possible way to go for Moroccan Microcredit Associations
    ISBN 978-3-8382-0494-9

11 Daniela Röttger
    Agricultural Finance for Smallholder Farmers
    Rethinking Traditional Microfinance Risk and Cost Management Approaches
    ISBN 978-3-8382-0745-2

Daniela Röttger

AGRICULTURAL FINANCE FOR SMALLHOLDER FARMERS

Rethinking Traditional Microfinance Risk and Cost Management Approaches

ibidem-Verlag
Stuttgart

Bibliografische Information der Deutschen Nationalbibliothek
Die Deutsche Nationalbibliothek verzeichnet diese Publikation in der
Deutschen Nationalbibliografie; detaillierte bibliografische Daten sind im
Internet über http://dnb.d-nb.de abrufbar.

Bibliographic information published by the Deutsche Nationalbibliothek
Die Deutsche Nationalbibliothek lists this publication in the Deutsche Nationalbibliografie;
detailed bibliographic data are available in the Internet at http://dnb.d-nb.de.

∞

Gedruckt auf alterungsbeständigem, säurefreien Papier
Printed on acid-free paper

ISSN: 2190-2291

ISBN-13: 978-3-8382-0745-2

© *ibidem*-Verlag
Stuttgart 2015

Alle Rechte vorbehalten

Das Werk einschließlich aller seiner Teile ist urheberrechtlich geschützt. Jede Verwertung außerhalb der engen Grenzen des Urheberrechtsgesetzes ist ohne Zustimmung des Verlages unzulässig und strafbar. Dies gilt insbesondere für Vervielfältigungen, Übersetzungen, Mikroverfilmungen und elektronische Speicherformen sowie die Einspeicherung und Verarbeitung in elektronischen Systemen.

All rights reserved. No part of this publication may be reproduced, stored in or introduced into a retrieval system, or transmitted, in any form, or by any means (electronic, mechanical, photocopying, recording or otherwise) without the prior written permission of the publisher. Any person who does any unauthorized act in relation to this publication may be liable to criminal prosecution and civil claims for damages.

Printed in Germany

Foreword

It is a great privilege and honor to write this foreword for this outstanding volume by Daniela Röttger, who won the 2013 University Meets Microfinance (UMM) award.

Since its creation in 2008, the Grameen Crédit Agricole Microfinance Foundation has the objective to support MFIs in rural areas and agriculture finance, with a strong focus on Sub-Sahara Africa. Established as a unique alliance between the Bangladeshi Grameen Trust and the French bank Crédit Agricole SA, the Foundation has the mission to contribute to the fight against poverty by supporting microfinance institutions (MFIs) and Social Business enterprises.

After 6 years, the Foundation is proud to have a partnership with 45 MFIs in 20 countries, more than half of them in Africa. Together these MFIs serve more than 2,3 million clients, of which 83% live in rural areas. Nevertheless, the proportion of their portfolio dedicated to agricultural finance is less than 30%. Taking into account our effort to find MFIs that finance agricultural activities, this figure is disappointingly low. And it clearly illustrates that many MFIs are still reluctant to finance agricultural activities due to the perceived high costs and risks, even though microfinance has, in general, successfully paved the way for offering financial services to low-income populations. In that context one question remains open: how to encourage MFIs to engage more in financing agricultural activities for small farmers. The research from Daniela Röttger clearly provides some concrete answers by providing a comprehensive analysis of the issue.

Especially in Sub-Sahara Africa, a continent where small farms account for 80% of the agricultural economy and where 70% of the poor work in agriculture, the challenge of financing smallholder farmers remains crucial. The research of Daniela can be very useful for all stakeholders interested to engage more in that field as it provides insights into how MFIs can successfully manage the risks of financing agricultural activities of smallholder farmers through adapted loan features and lending procedures.

The research thereby systematically links theory with practice. It offers a comprehensive overview of risk and costs of agricultural microfinance and theoretically analyses the extent to which traditional microfinance risk management approaches are able to mitigate these agricultural risks. But more importantly, it offers practical insights into the experiences of MFIs that already offer finance for agricultural activities by interviewing eight MFIs in four countries in East and West

Africa (Uganda, Kenya, Benin, Cameroon). By identifying their loan features and lending mechanism specific to agricultural lending, the empirical research provides concrete examples of the microfinance mechanism that work in agricultural lending and the ones that need to be adapted and thereby underpins the theoretical analysis.

The main contribution of this research is, however, the comprehensive and systematic comparison of the microfinance approaches to manage risks versus the agricultural microfinance approaches, with a summary of the "successful" approaches to manage risk in agricultural microfinance. All main issues have been clearly identified and analyzed, such as the need to adapt loan features to agricultural production cycles (interest rate, duration, repayment schedule), to have qualified staff with sound agricultural knowledge, to perceive and analyze farmers as a part of an agricultural value chain and to introduce innovation like agri-microinsurance and new technology to mitigate costs and reduce risks.

Even though a deeper analysis of the portfolio quality of the studied MFIs, which is a key element for all investors, is missing in the research, the analysis succeeds in demonstrating that MFIs are able to provide relevant services to small farmers and finance their agricultural activities, if there is a strong commitment at the highest level of the institution and the willingness to adapt the methodologies, to innovate and to take well-balanced risk. The Grameen Crédit Agricole Microfinance Foundation can fully share this conclusion based on its own field experience with its partners. However, financing agricultural activities for small farmers is not the sole responsibility of MFIs. It will only be successful with a strong commitment from all stakeholders, especially regulators and funders, which also need to adapt their methodology, approach, services and products. Only then have MFIs the best chances to succeed with their agricultural lending efforts.

This thesis is a concrete example of how very good practical, field based research can help practitioners and the sector in general to better understand some of their key challenges and to open new opportunities for development and innovation. The work of University Meets Microfinance in supporting such master students in their field research and providing them with the opportunity to disseminate their work is unique and extremely relevant.

I am convinced that the readers will share my pleasure of reading this work to better understand how microfinance institutions can contribute to sustain a successful agricultural microfinance business for the benefit of small farmers.

Philippe Guichandut , Paris, November 5th 2014
Head of Development and Technical Assistance at the Grameen Crédit Agricole Microfinance Foundation

Table of Contents

List of Figures 9

List of Tables 9

List of Abbreviations 11

1 Introduction 15
   1.1 The relevance of agricultural finance for increasing
       smallholder farmers' productivity 15
   1.2 Purpose and outline of the paper 17
   1.3 Methodology 19

2 Terminology and historical background of agricultural finance for
   smallholder farmers 23
   2.1 Terminology 23
       2.1.1 Microfinance, rural finance, and agricultural finance 23
       2.1.2 Smallholder farmers: definition and financial needs 27
   2.2 The history of agricultural finance for smallholder farmers:
       a change of underlying principles 31
       2.2.1 Old paradigm: subsidized agricultural credit 31
       2.2.2 Emergence of a new paradigm 34
       *2.2.3 Linking the new paradigm and agricultural finance for
            smallholder farmers 35*

3 Risks and costs of agricultural lending for smallholder farmers 37
   3.1 (Credit) risks specific to agricultural lending for smallholder farmers 37
   3.2 Costs specific to agricultural lending for smallholder farmers 42

4 Traditional microfinance risk and cost management approaches:
   do they work for smallholder farmers? 45
   4.1 Loan product design for risk mitigation in traditional microfinance 46
   4.2 Loan assessment and monitoring for risk mitigation in traditional
       microfinance 52
   4.3 Reducing transaction costs in traditional microfinance 57

5 Interim conclusion 59

Table of Contents

6 Overview of interviewed MFIs and their agricultural lending strategies.... 61
6.1 Indicators and agricultural loan products of interviewed MFIs 61
6.2 Commercial banks 65
6.3 Microfinance companies 68
6.4 Membership-based financial institutions 72

7 Risk mitigation through adapted loan products and lending procedures ... 79
7.1 Loan features of agricultural production loans 79
    7.1.2 Discussion of interest rates 94
7.2 Risk management through adapted lending procedures 106

8 Further strategies to reduce risks and transaction costs in agricultural lending to smallholder farmers 117
8.1 Qualified staff with agricultural backgrounds 117
8.2 Value chain finance 119
8.3 Cooperation with external actors 125
8.4 Cost-effective outreach to smallholder farmers 127

9 Conclusion 131

Bibliography 135

Annex 143

List of Figures

Figure 1: Defining agricultural finance for smallholder farmers 24
Figure 2: Effects of different loan terms and repayment schedules 50
Figure 3: Farm gate price of seed cotton 2007–2013 104
Figure 4: External value chain finance for cotton smallholders in Benin 123
Figure 5: M-Kesho money flow and charges 129

List of Tables

Table 1: Overview of the interviewed MFIs 20
Table 2: Comparison of paradigms of agricultural finance for smallholder farmers 32
Table 3: Micro-finance risk categories 37
Table 4: Typical loan features of traditional microfinance credits 46
Table 5: Credit risk mitigation during loan assessment and monitoring in traditional microfinance 52
Table 6: Traditional microfinance requirements and agricultural investments ... 60
Table 7: Comparison of indicators of interviewed MFIs in 2011* 62
Table 8: Overview of agricultural loan portfolio and loan products of interviewed MFIs* 63
Table 9: Loan features of short-term agricultural loans of interviewed MFIs..... 80
Table 10: Loan features of medium-/long-term agricultural loans of interviewed MFIs 81
Table 11: Comparison of interest rates of agricultural and commercial loans 96
Table 12: Short-term loans—effective vs. quoted interest rate 99
Table 13: Medium-/long-term loans—effective vs. quoted interest rate 100
Table 14: Costs of cotton production in SSA 103
Table 15: Comparison of EIRs: highest vs. lowest; unsubsidized vs. subsidized 105
Table 16: Additional income at different interest rates and farm gate prices 105
Table 17: Comparison of loan assessment and monitoring 108
Table 18: Educational background of agricultural loan officers 119

List of Abbreviations

aBi Trust	Agricultural Business Initiative Trust
ACCI	Adaption to Climate Change and Insurance
ADAF	Appropriate Development for Africa Foundation
AFD	Agence Francaise de Développement
AFRACA	African Rural and Agricultural Credit Association
AGRA	Alliance for a Green Revolution
AIC	Association Interprofessionelle du Coton
AU	African Union
BMZ	Bundesministerium für wirtschaftliche Zusammenarbeit und Entwicklung (German Federal Ministry for Economic Cooperation and Development)
CB	Commercial Bank
CeCPA	Centre Communale pour la Promotion d'Agriculture
CeRPA	Centre Regionale pour la Promotion d'Agriculture
CGAP	Consultative Group to Assist the Poor
CLCAM	Caisses Locales de Crédit Agricole Mutual
CNCA	Caisse Nationale de Crédit Agricole
COMPACI	Competitive African Cotton Initiative
CRDB	Centenary Rural Development Bank
CSPR	Centrale de Sécurisation de Paiement et de Recouvrement
DEG	Deutsche Investitions- und Entwicklungsgesellschaft (German Investment and Development Corporation)
DFID	Department for International Development
EIR	Effective Interest Rate

12 List of Abbrevations

FAO	Food and Agriculture Organization
FECECAM	Faîtière des Caisses d'Epargne et de Crédit Agricole Mutuel
GDP	Gross Domestic Product
GDPRD	Global Donor Platform for Rural Development
GIGA	German Institute for Global and Area Studies
GIZ	Deutsche Gesellschaft für Internationale Zusammenarbeit (German Society for International Cooperation)
GLP	Gross Loan Portfolio
GTZ	Deutsche Gesellschaft für technische Zusammenarbeit (German Technical Cooperation)
HH	Household
HYV	High Yielding Varieties
IAASTD	International Assessment of Agricultural Knowledge, Science and Technology for Development
IBLF	International Business Leaders Forum
IFAD	International Fund for Agricultural Development
IFPRI	International Food Policy Research Institute
IIED	International Institute for Environment and Development
i	Interest rate
KfW	Kreditanstalt für Wiederaufbau (Bank for Reconstruction)
KDA	K-Rep Development Agency
LACE	Loan Application and Credit Evaluation
MBFI	Membership-based Financial Institution
MC^2	Mutuelles Communautaires de Croissance
MFC	Microfinance Company
MFI	Microfinance Institution

MFW4A	Making Finance Work for Africa
MoA	Ministry of Agriculture
NGO	Non-Governmental Organization
NPL	Non-performing Loan
OSS	Operational self-sufficiency
PAD	Projet d'Appui aux Etablissements de Microfinance de Développement
PAR	Portfolio at Risk
PTI	Pricing Transparency Index
RUCREF	Rural Credit Finance Company
SACCO	Savings and Credit Co-operative
SADC	Southern African Development Community
SDC	Swiss Agency for Development Cooperation
SSA	Sub-Saharan Africa
UCA	Ugandan Coffee Farmer Alliance
UNEP	United Nations Environment Programme
UNIDO	United Nations Industrial Development Organization
URCLCAM	Unions Régionales des Caisses Locales de Crédit Agricole Mutuel
WOCCU	World Council of Credit Unions

All dollar amounts are US dollars unless otherwise indicated.

1 Introduction

1.1 The relevance of agricultural finance for increasing smallholder farmers' productivity

Over the last decade, the international development discussion rediscovered the importance of smallholder agricultural development for poverty reduction and food security in Sub-Saharan Africa (SSA). It became obvious that poverty cannot be reduced without addressing smallholder agricultural development on a continent where smallholder farms account for 80% of the agricultural economy, 70% of the poor work in agriculture and yet "a staggering one out of three is undernourished" (Haggblade et al. 2010, 3; IAASTD 2009b, 6)[1]. Moreover, agriculture plays a key role in the overall economies of most SSA countries in terms of standard economic indicators with its contribution to the gross domestic product (GDP), foreign exchange earnings, and number of people employed (Dorward et al. 2009, 5ff.). Here, agriculture not only accounts for about 25–30% of the combined GDP and for over half of total export earnings but also for 65% of SSA's full-time employment (IAASTD 2009a, 2; Yumkella et al. 2011, 17). Increasing smallholder farmers' agricultural productivity can, therefore, be a powerful tool for spearheading broad-based income gains for both farmers as well as non-farmers. Higher production generates more income among smallholders[2] and their increased purchasing power can promote a diversification of the local economies by creating jobs in commerce, small business, and handcraft (Wolz 2005, ii). Consequently, Birner/Resnick (2010, 1442ff.) state that there has been no example of mass poverty reduction in modern history that was not based on increased productivity on small family farms. Smallholder agriculture is, however, not only of interest to donors and their poverty reduction strategies. Multinational buyers of agricultural products also started to recognize the importance of smallholder agriculture. Faced with an increasing global demand for agricultural commodities and growing consumer preferences for sustainable products, leading buyers have increased their share of agricultural products sourced from smallholder farmers (Carroll et al. 2012, 5).

---

[1] Please note that literature references written before the punctuation at the end of a sentence only refer to the previous sentence, while references made after the punctuation refer to the entire previous paragraph.

[2] The terms *smallholder farmer* and *smallholder* are used interchangeably here and in the following.

Even though many agricultural specialists see a significant potential to increase the productivity of smallholder agriculture in SSA (Haggblade et al. 2010, 5; Brüntrup 2011, Klerk et al. 2011, 3), multiple constraints exist. Currently smallholder agriculture in most SSA countries is characterized by low yields and low product quality and lags far behind in terms of productivity compared to other world regions. The constraints to a more profitable agriculture are manifold and often beyond the control of the farmers. Among them are a negative influence of the worldwide agricultural policies; low public sector expenditure on agriculture; poor rural infrastructure (roads and communication); uncertain legal environment (e.g. modern and traditional rules on land); very thin or deficient markets for (financial) services and agricultural inputs (quality seeds and agrochemicals) and outputs (marketing of agricultural products); as well as inadequate extension services, water management, and research and development support. These challenges often reinforce each other and lead to a generally hostile business environment, making profitable smallholder agricultural difficult. Smallholder farmers have to struggle to access basic services required for profitable production (adequate supply of high-quality inputs, extension services, and reliable markets to sell their products). Furthermore, many farmers lack the managerial and/or technical skills as well as the internal capital resources to produce regular surpluses for the market. These illustrations clearly demonstrate that agricultural development and increased agricultural productivity require a joint effort by different stakeholders and different strategies and approaches. (Dorward et al. 2009, 7ff.; Haggblade et al. 2010, 6ff.)

Providing access to capital and other financial products is one important part in the overall strategy to enhance the productivity of smallholders and improve their livelihood. Even though "loans cannot substitute for appropriate technology, input supplies, and access to remunerative markets" (Meyer 2011, 6), borrowed funds can assist farmers with access to markets to invest in new farming technologies, high-quality inputs (e.g. quality seeds, fertilizers, agrochemicals) or mechanization and equipment (e.g. oxen, plough, sprayer). Adequate access to borrowed capital and other financial services can thus enable farmers to produce more for the market, improve their food security, and raise their agricultural returns (Klerk et al. 2011, 3). In addition, other financial services like insurance products and saving possibilities can lower the risk of external shocks, smoothen cyclical cash flows of farmers and help them to manage their farm as a viable business.

While microfinance institutions (MFIs) were successful in developing techniques to provide financial services to low-income clients without traditional collateral, rural areas and smallholder farmers in particular are still underserved by the microfinance industry (Morvant-Roux 2009, 189). MFIs are reluctant to move into rural areas due to the perceived high risks and costs associated with lending to agricultural clients.

It can thus be concluded that:

> "financial services will probably not, on their own, bring about greater investment in productivity or income from agriculture or any other rural enterprise. However, if such improvements are insufficient on their own to ensure progress, they are clearly a sine qua non for such gains. *Yet, of the many pre-conditions for agriculture and rural development, the provision of financial services remain among the most poorly understood.*"
> (Klerk et al. 2011, 4; emphasis added)

1.2 Purpose and outline of the paper

This paper will shed more light on the provision of agricultural finance to smallholder farmers in SSA. It will thereby be guided by the following research question:

How can microfinance institutions adapt their traditional loan features and lending procedures to mitigate credit risk and manage transaction costs when providing agricultural finance for smallholder farmers?

This research question defines the scope of this paper: the focus is on MFIs' (internal) procedures to mitigate credit risks and transactions costs for agriculture. The research question implies that traditional microfinance risk management techniques (e.g. their loan features and lending procedures), if applied as is, are not well suited for agricultural investments of smallholder farmers and thus need to be adapted to the particulars of agricultural smallholder lending.

While there is abundant literature on general credit risk management for MFIs, very little research has been done on the specific management of agriculture-related credit risks.[3] Research on rural finance and/or smallholder (agriculture) finance is often limited to explanations of why these financial services are non-existent in rural areas, that is, it is limited to descriptions of the respective risks and

---

[3] The author is only aware of two exceptions, namely Christen/Pearce 2005 and Klein et al. 1999.

costs of agricultural micro-lending. Additionally, while a number of one-off case studies exist (e.g. presentations at conferences), which use the example of a single MFI offering finance for smallholder farmers to show that it is possible to do so, the information provided by such cases are limited in nature, making a comparison between case studies impractical.

The present paper is an attempt to focus specifically on the management of agriculture-related risks and costs in microfinance. After a brief outline of the specific risks and costs of agricultural lending as found in existing literature (Chapter 3), Chapter 4 will examine traditional microfinance (credit) risk and cost management approaches with regard to their appropriateness for smallholder agriculture. Based on this analysis, Chapters 6–8 will provide empirical insights into the topic. Eight MFIs providing agricultural finance to smallholder farmers in East and West Africa were interviewed from June to September 2011 and asked about their loan products for smallholders as well as their lending techniques to mitigate the risks and costs of lending to this target group. After presenting their diverse institutional backgrounds and specific business strategies and approaches to agricultural finance for smallholders in Chapter 6, this paper will focus on the loan products and lending procedures in Chapters 7 and 8. The analysis will concentrate on which of the traditional microfinance approaches MFIs are using within their lending activities for smallholders and which ones they adapted, changed, or added to be able to mitigate the additional risks and costs associated with agricultural finance for smallholders as depicted in Chapter 3.

Besides drawing on the conducted interviews, the paper also refers to two other important studies dealing with the aspect of agricultural microfinance for smallholder farmers. The first is entitled "Better Practices in Agricultural Lending" and was published in 1999 by Klein et al. Drawing on case studies of three MFIs in Thailand, Peru, and El Salvador, it analyses how microfinance techniques in urban areas could provide models for agricultural production lending. A more recent study entitled "Managing Risk and Designing Products for Agricultural Microfinance: Features of an Emerging Model" was conducted by Christen/Pearce (2005). They studied a total of 30 MFIs worldwide that successfully lend to smallholder farmers. They then develop 10 features and suggested that a combination of a substantial number of these features contributes to a well-performing agricultural portfolio. The features range from recommendations for lending techniques (e.g. Feature 2: Combine character-based lending techniques with technical criteria in selecting borrowers, setting loan terms, and enforcing repayments) over suggestions to offering specific products (e.g. Feature 3: Offer savings mechanism) to general proposals (e.g. Feature 10: To succeed, agricultural microfinance must be insulated from political interference). A third study on this topic entitled, "Assessing and Managing Credit-risk in Agricultural Lending" was conducted by the World Bank. It analyses 17 financial institutions in nine countries.[4] Unfortunately, the study has not yet been published and the rather general conclusions that have been presented at conferences are not far reaching.[5] While the third study unfortunately cannot be taken into account, the other two studies are drawn upon for the present paper and used to support or confront the finding of this paper as applicable. While the first study does not include MFIs from SSA, the second one does, but as MFIs were not named and only some were disclosed within short case studies, the exact number of African MFIs within the sample is not known.

1.3 Methodology

This paper and the necessary empirical research was developed and conducted with the support of the German Development Finance Institution (DEG) and their Competitive African Cotton Initiative (COMPACI). COMPACI's goal is to enable smallholder cotton farmers to earn higher incomes through their cotton production by sustainably raising their productivity, providing market access through the label Cotton made in Africa (CmiA), improving soil fertility and improving access to microfinance among others.[6]

From June to September 2011, qualitative, semi-structured interviews were conducted with different MFIs in four countries, namely Uganda, Kenya, Benin, and Cameroon. A range of MFIs with different institutional backgrounds were chosen to ensure a broad picture of agricultural lending to smallholder farmers. The different institutions include: (1) membership-based financial institutions (MBFIs) (e.g. credit unions and savings and credit co-operatives) that offer a range of financial products solely to their members; (2) microfinance companies (MFCs) purely concentrating on micro-clients and the provision of microfinance services; and (3)

---

[4] Unfortunately, the study does not name the included countries. Only some countries were disclosed within short case studies, which indicate that some African MFIs were included.
[5] Also upon request and after some e-mail exchange, only a rough two-page summary that is not to be cited was provided.
[6] Additional information on COMPACI can be found at COMPACI (2013).

commercial banks (CBs) offering microfinance and agricultural finance for smallholder farmers as part of their overall banking portfolio. The MFCs interviewed were all spin-offs of non-governmental organizations (NGOs) and now trying to reach financial sustainability as standalone institutions. Table 1 depicts the interviewed MFIs, their respective institutional background, as well as the country in which they operate. A detailed presentation of the MFIs will be given in Chapter 6.

Table 1: Overview of the interviewed MFIs

	CB	MFC	MBFI
Kenya	(1) Equity Bank	(3) Faulu (4) Juhudi Kilimo Limited	
Uganda	(2) Centenary Rural Development Bank (CRDB)	(5) Rural Credit Finance Company Limited (RUCREF)	(6) Agaru Savings and Credit Co-operative (SACCO)
Benin			(7) Caisses Locales de Crédit Agricole Mutual (CLCAM) Kuandé and Pehunco
Cameroon			(8) MC²/ADAF

Source: own table.

Employees who were actively involved in agricultural lending for smallholder farmers within these institutions, either in the head office designing loan products for smallholder farmers and overseeing the agricultural business of the respective MFI (e.g. Agribusiness general manager) or "in the field" actively engaged with smallholders in day-to-day business (e.g. agricultural loan officer), were chosen for the interviews.

In Benin and Cameroon, the focus of research was on specific programmes supporting the agricultural lending activities of either CLCAMs or MC²s, and therefore employees involved in the respective programme were also interviewed. In Benin, the two interviewed CLCAMs in Kuandé and Pehunco set up a credit scheme for cotton smallholder farmers in collaboration with the COMPACI programme, and thus employees of the COMPACI programme were interviewed. MC²s in Cameroon are supported and controlled by an NGO called Appropriate Development for Africa Foundation (ADAF).[7] ADAF also supports MC²s to implement a government-funded programme called Projet d'Appui aux Etablissements

---

[7] Further information on the structure of the MC² network (Mutuelles Communautaires de Croissance) and the role of ADAF can be found in Chapter 6.

de Microfinance de Développement (PAD), which intends to increase agricultural lending activities of MC²s and was the focus of the conducted research for this paper. Interviews were, therefore, conducted with several staff members of ADAF. Additionally, experts and consultants working in the field of agricultural finance for smallholder farmers were interviewed in all four countries. An overview of interview partners is given in Annex A.

MFIs were chosen based on their different institutional backgrounds as well as their accessibility, as it is not easy to get in touch with MFIs involved in agricultural finance of smallholder farmers based on literature review and Internet searches, especially when working from Germany.[8] In the case of CLCAMs and MC²s in Benin and Cameroon access was possible through COMPACI. A Conference on the research topic in Kampala/Uganda in June 2011 ("Zipping Finance and Farming in Africa—Harnessing the Continent's Potential") opened the possibility to contact most of the Ugandan and Kenyan MFIs interviewed for the purpose of this paper. Equity Bank Nairobi, Kenya was chosen as one of the few well-known MFIs involved in agricultural finance for smallholder farmers. Even though this approach was quite successful and a number of different MFIs with diverse institutional backgrounds and experiences could be interviewed, it was not possible to choose MFIs according to their overall performance [e.g. portfolio at risk (PAR) or non-performing loans (NPLs) in agriculture]. Additionally, the sample set cannot claim to be representative as the number of MFIs is too small and MFIs were neither selected randomly nor on the basis of specific indicators.

Length and intensity varied among the 18 interviews used for this paper. The researcher was based for a period of 2 weeks in Benin within the COMPACI project collaborating with CLCAMs and another 2 weeks in Cameroon at ADAF. This allowed specific issues to be re-discussed with the interview partners as well as for more detailed information to be gathered. Also at Equity Bank and Agaru SACCO several interviews were conducted allowing for cross-checking information. At the other MFIs, only one interview was conducted. Each interview lasted 1.5–2 hours and was recorded. In addition to the interview transcriptions, additional information on the respective MFIs was collected and analysed, for example, financial statements, reports, articles, etc. Interviews were transcribed mostly word for word and sometimes as a detailed protocol based on the recorded interview. Filler words,

---

[8] Many MFIs cannot be found in literature, web pages are often outdated, telephone numbers not provided, and e-mail requests go unanswered.

breaks in conversation, and non-verbal communication were not documented. The interviews were conducted in French and English, neither of which is the native language of the researcher. For this reason, a single word that could not be understood is marked by "(x)" and several words by "(xx)".

Interviews were analysed using the method of qualitative content analysis by Gläser/Laudel (2009). Different categories and sub-categories were established based on the theoretical research as well as on the additional background knowledge gained during the interviews. Interviews and additional literature were then screened and encoded with MAXQDA according to these categories. Sentences and text passages were extracted with their references allowing for traceability and allocated to a single category. It should be noted that this process is already part of the interpretation, as the researcher decided on the categories as well as on the allocation of text passages to specific categories (Gläser/Laudel 2009, 199ff.).

The main limitations have already been mentioned. First, they are the lack of representativeness of institutions, and secondly the limited numbers of interviews per MF, especially in East Africa. Cross-checking the information from one employee of an MFI with statements made by other employees of the same institution would have increased the reliability of data. However, all MFIs were rather busy and had limited time and resources for several interviews. An attempt to set off this limitation as far as possible was made by cross-checking information provided in annual reports, financial statements, and articles on the respective MFIs. It is still possible that some information from the interviews were misunderstood, for which the author takes full responsibility.

2 Terminology and historical background of agricultural finance for smallholder farmers

There is a growing body of literature dealing with aspects related to rural (micro-) finance, agricultural (micro-) finance, and agricultural value chain finance. These aspects are all related to agricultural finance for smallholder farmers and are sometimes even used as synonyms. However, there are major differences between these different terms and it is important not to confuse them. Section 2.1, therefore, defines these terms and thereby also establishes the scope of this paper. Additionally, the term smallholder farmer will be defined including the financial needs of this specific group of interest. Section 2.2 then provides an overview of the major lessons learned from the experiences with subsidized credit programmes and agricultural development banks in the 1950s and 1960s and summarizes the main principles of today's financial system approach, which sets the frame for the provision of agricultural finance for smallholder farmers at present.

2.1 Terminology

2.1.1 Microfinance, rural finance, and agricultural finance

The diagram in Figure 1 illustrates the terminology used in this paper. The striped area represents the main topic: agricultural finance for smallholder farmers, which is situated at the intersection of microfinance, rural, and agricultural finance.

Figure 1: Defining agricultural finance for smallholder farmers

[Venn diagram showing: financial sector (outer), containing rural finance and microfinance circles, with agricultural finance overlapping rural finance and microfinance; the intersection of agricultural finance and microfinance labeled "agricultural finance for smallholder farmers"]

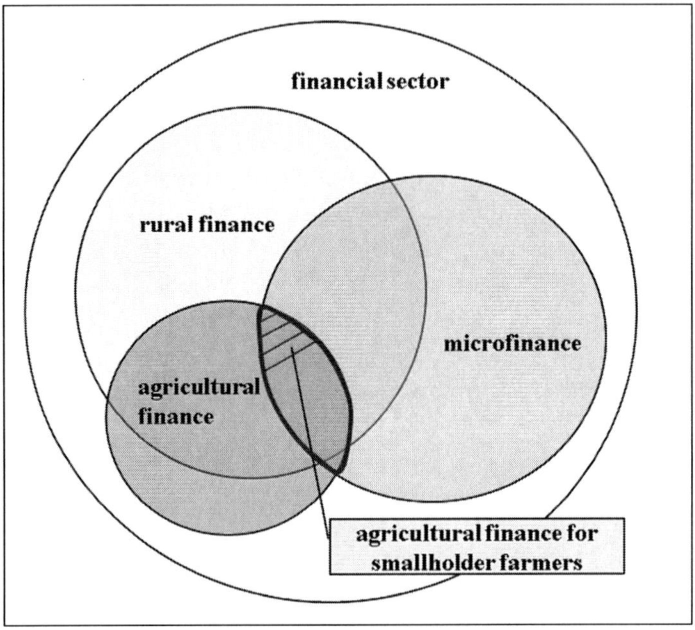

Source: own figure based on Pearce (2003, 1).

Microfinance refers to a broad array of financial products (savings, payment transfers, credit, and insurance) specifically designed to meet the needs of low-income households and small-scale businesses, both in urban and rural areas. This target group is not served by traditional CBs because they are not considered to be viable customers. (CGAP 2013; Pearce 2003, 1; Meyer 2011, 3)

Microfinance services can be provided by different types of institutions. Per definition, any institution or individual that provides financial services to low-income clients offers microfinance. This paper, however, only refers to formal and semi-formal MFIs with the term MFI. Formal MFIs are subject to banking regulations and supervision and provide finance to the above-defined micro-clients. These include public or private CBs, some microfinance companies, and insurance companies. Three of the interviewed MFIs belong to this group: Equity Bank and CRDB are private CBs that also target micro-clients with part of their portfolio, while Faulu is a formerly NGO-based microfinance company that acquired a deposit-taking licence and is thus regulated by the central bank, just as the rest of the formal MFIs.

Semi-formal MFIs are recognized financial institutions, but are not subject to the same legislations as formal banks. In many countries, they are licensed and supervised by another government authority instead. Examples include credit unions, which are often supervised by a bureau in charge of co-operatives, and microfinance companies or NGOs that solely provide credit, since they are often legally registered entities that are subject to some form of supervision or reporting requirements. Registered village banks, self-help groups, and savings clubs are also often considered as part of the semi-formal sector. (Ledgerwood 1999, 12ff.) Five of the interviewed MFIs belong to this group: CLCAMs, Agaru SACCO, and MC²s are membership-based credit unions, whereas Juhudi Kilimo and RUCREF are formerly NGO-based microfinance companies that solely provide credit.

Rural finance describes all financial services provided to a heterogeneous rural population of all income levels through all kinds of financial service providers (Nagarajan/Meyer 2005, 1). Other than microfinance, which is defined through its target group, rural finance is defined through its location. The term ***rural microfinance*** can be used for the combination of the two, hence the provision of microfinance services in rural areas (represented by the intersection of microfinance and rural finance in Figure 1). MFIs are often based in rural town centres. Therefore, rural microfinance often does not target farming households, but small entrepreneurial activities in rural towns. (FinMark Trust 2011; Beck et al. 2011, 92; Adesina 2010, 74)

Agricultural finance is mostly referred to as financial services used by the agricultural sector for farming as well as farm-related activities along the entire value chain, for example, input supply, agricultural production, processing, wholesaling, and marketing. Besides working capital or asset loans for farmers, traders, or processors, it can also include crop or livestock insurance or leasing agricultural equipment. (Meyer 2011, 3; MFW4A 2012; Brüntrup 2008, 4; Andrews/MEDA 2006, 3) The respective definition uses the activity for which finance is provided for (e.g. agriculture) as defining feature.

A conference paper of the African Union (AU) and Making Finance Work for Africa (MFW4A) proposes a wider definition and defines agricultural finance as "finance related to agriculture-specific risk" (AU/MFW4A 2011, 12).[9] This has important consequences when applying it to reality. A financial institution that uses the first definition would offer an agricultural loan with specific features that fit the agricultural production cycle (e.g. offering repayment after harvest) only for farm-related activities, for example, the purchase of inputs. A financial institution applying the latter definition, on the other hand, would also offer these loan products with adapted features for other loan needs of a primarily agricultural household, for example, the school loan of a smallholder farmer would fall under agricultural finance and would thus be offered at the same conditions as an input loan. Both definitions are important for this paper, as one interviewed MFI defines agricultural finance based on agriculture-specific risk, while all other interviewed MFIs use the other definition.

Independent of the above definition, agricultural finance will mostly be located in rural areas. However, large processing facilities or agribusinesses are also present in urban areas. (Meyer 2011, 3) Agricultural finance is offered by financial institutions, as well as by value chain actors themselves, for example, when an input supplier provides credit to a farmer. The latter is called internal *agricultural value chain finance* and is not covered by this paper, as the focus of this paper is on the provision of financial services through financial institutions. Section 8.2 illustrates that some financial institutions cooperate with agricultural value chain actors and provide agricultural finance based on existing value chain links, for example, a contract between a smallholder farmer and a trusted buyer. This lowers the risks and costs of financial institutions to lend to smallholder farmers and can be referred to as external value chain finance (Miller/Jones 2010, 2).

The red-framed bold area in Figure 1 illustrates the overlap of agricultural finance and microfinance and is, therefore, called *agricultural microfinance*. It describes the provision of financial services for farming, farm-related activities, or activities with agricultural-related risk for low-income clients, which could be smallholder farmers as well as small-input providers or small buyers and traders of agricultural products.

Agricultural finance for smallholder farmers is a subsection of agricultural microfinance and marked as a striped area in Figure 1. Applying the narrow definition of agricultural finance, it refers to the provision of financial services for agri-

---

[9] This wider definition was suggested by Michael Jainzik, who works for the German Bank for Reconstruction (KfW).

cultural activities of smallholder farmers, for example, working capital or asset loans for agricultural production or weather insurance. Using the wider definition it would also cover other financial needs of smallholder farmers (e.g. consumption or emergency credits, savings, insurances) as long as their main household income derives from agriculture and is, therefore, prone to agricultural-related risk. Chapter 6 shows that one interviewed MFI (Equity Bank) uses this wider definition, whereas all other interviewed MFIs solely apply the term *agricultural finance for smallholder farmers* to their agricultural loan products targeted at financing or insuring agricultural production.

2.1.2 Smallholder farmers: definition and financial needs

When looking at definitions of smallholder farmers used in publications of international agricultural organizations such as the Food and Agriculture Organization (FAO), International Food Policy Research Institute (IFPRI), International Fund for Agricultural Development (IFAD), and United Nations Environment Programme (UNEP) one can see that a unique and universally accepted definition of a smallholder farmer does not exist. The following, therefore, draws a general picture of a smallholder by resorting to the common features of all definitions.

Overall, all definitions describe smallholders as producers of agricultural food and non-food products that are marginalized relative to other farmers in terms of one or several features, for example, land size and/or land quality, capital and assets, access to technology and information, the use of external inputs, and the number of (employed) workers (IFAD/UNEP 2013, 10; Dixon et al. 2004; Chamberlin 2007, 3ff.). Land size is the feature most commonly employed to define smallholder farmers. Large differences in general land potential and soil quality in different agro-ecological zones and different countries, however, make it difficult to solely use land size as criterion. While a farmer in a favourable area with high population density might be defined as smallholder when s/he cultivates less than 1 ha, another farmer cultivating 10 ha or more in a semi-arid area with low soil quality would also qualify as smallholder in terms of other marginalizing factors. (IFAD/UNEP 2013, 10; Dixon et al. 2004)

In addition to the above features, most smallholder farmers are also characterized by their dependency on family labour, diverse sources of household incomes including significant off-farm earnings and the cultivation of low-risk, low-return crops with a significant share reserved for their own consumption

(IFAD/UNEP 2013, 10; Dixon et al. 2004; Chamberlin 2007, 3ff.; Doran et al. 2009 13ff.). Doran et al. (2009, 13ff.) describe these patterns as rational risk mitigation strategies against economic and climatic shock such as drought, heavy and/or untimely rainfall, variable soil conditions, pest and disease outbreaks, and volatility in market prices for agricultural products that can lead to income losses. In the absence of adequate risk mitigation mechanism (e.g. weather insurance) and/or other supporting services (e.g. adequate extension services, infrastructure, access to market or storage facilities, etc.) and/or a lack of managerial and technical skills (e.g. how to manage the farm as a business, how to improve soil fertility), smallholders try to reduce their overall household risk through diversifying their income sources across farm and non-farm activities. Within agricultural production they often favour to grow low-risk, low-return crops that do not require significant investment in expensive inputs, but are more robust even in unfavourable soil and weather conditions. This also minimizes their demand for external capital. Even though an investment in inputs could significantly increase smallholders' overall crop yields, many smallholders are reluctant to carry out such an investment due to the above-mentioned risks and would rather rely on the security of a sub-optimal food supply for basic household consumption and then market any surplus they might achieve. Finance alone is not sufficient to break this vicious cycle referred to as the "risk trap for subsistence smallholders" by Doran et al. (2009, 13). Joint efforts by various stakeholders and different strategies and approaches are also needed.

Before proceeding to the financial needs of smallholder farmers and the benefits financial services can bring about to productivity and an increase in income, a working definition of a smallholder farmer based on the above elaborations and adapted to the context of microfinance will be developed. The MFIs that were interviewed did not have a definition of smallholders themselves, but used some criteria as guideline during their loan assessment to choose eligible smallholders for their financial products. To access agricultural loans from the interviewed MFIs, the smallholders' main source of income needed to be agriculture. However, most MFIs required or expected diversification within the agricultural production, as well as some off-farm side income sources to decrease agriculture-related risks. Additionally, smallholders needed to have a commercial mind-set, meaning that they were not solely subsistence farmers that only sold their surplus to the market, but were actively growing crops for marketing and earning a living. Due to their lack of traditional collateral and their belonging to the low-income population, these smallholders fell under the microfinance section of the interviewed banks.

Based on the above elaborations, the definition of a smallholder farmer for this paper is therefore as follows: *A smallholder farmer is a commercial producer of food and non-food agricultural products that is marginalized relative to other farmers in terms of one or several features (e.g. land size and/ or land quality, capital and assets, access to technology and information, use of external inputs or number of (employed) workers) and has no adequate traditional collateral to access formal banking services.*

Even though "loans cannot substitute for appropriate technology, input supplies, and access to remunerative markets" (Meyer 2011, 6), a mix of complementary financial services both for farm and off-farm activities can assist smallholders to maximize the allocation of self-mobilized or borrowed capital and to manage foreseen and unforeseen risks (Doran et al. 2011, 14; Meyer 2011, 6; Klerk et al. 2011, 3; FinMark Trust 2011, 10). Borrowed funds can support farmers with access to inputs and markets to invest in new farming technologies, high-quality inputs (quality seeds, fertilizers, agrochemicals) or mechanization and equipment (oxen, plough, and sprayer). Additionally, other financial services can lower the risk of external shocks, smooth out cyclical cash flows, and help farmers to lead their farm as a viable business. Smallholders' needs for full banking services and not just for agricultural production loans is supported by a FinMark Trust sponsored study (FinMark Trust 2011).[10] It finds that savings, money transfer services, and credits are the most demanded components, whereas the demand for agricultural insurance is not yet widespread (FinMark Trust 2011, 10).

Without neglecting the importance of full banking services for smallholder farmers, the paper's focus is on agricultural production loans (especially short-term working capital and medium- and long-term asset finance) for smallholder farmers.[11] This is due to the fact that most microfinance risks specific to agriculture fall

---

[10] The study tries to calculate the actual demand for rural financial services in six countries of the Southern African Development Community (SADC), e.g. Botswana, Malawi, Mozambique, South Africa, Zambia, and Zimbabwe.

[11] A detailed description of financial services demanded by smallholder farmers is offered by Dorward et al. (2011, 14ff.), AU/MFW4A (2011, 28ff.), Doran et al. (2009, 14ff.), and Goodland et al. (1999, 6ff.).

under credit risk as will be explained in Chapter 3.[12] Consumption credits are also important for smallholder farmers, but only fall under the wider definition of agricultural finance (e.g. finance prone to agricultural risk), which is solely applied by one interviewed MFI.[13]

Short-term, working capital loans for agricultural production (up to 12 months) are used for "current expenditures that occur in the normal course of the business (...) [or] short-term assets to be used within one year" (Ledgerwood 1999, 136). They mostly finance seasonal inputs such as seeds, fertilizer, agro-chemicals, feeds, hired labour, or veterinary services for livestock (Doran et al. 2009, 14; AU/MFW4A 2011, 29ff.).

Medium- and long-term loans and/or leases for agricultural production (loan period of more than 12 months) are mostly fixed asset loans and finance

> "assets that are used over time in the business (...) [and] usually have a life span of more than one year. (...) the productive activity does not directly use up the fixed asset (...), its impact upon profitability is felt over a longer period of time." (Ledgerwood 1999, 136)

Fixed asset loans are often used for purchasing agricultural equipment to enhance productivity (e.g. farm machinery, water supply and irrigation equipment, farm forestry development) or for investing in livestock activities (livestock, fencing, machinery, ponds and cages for fish farming).[14] (AU/MFW4A 2011, 29ff.; Doran et al. 2009, 14)

Consumption and emergency credits are used by smallholders for their livelihood protection. Due to the seasonality of agriculture, cash constraints often occur shortly before the harvest and selling period, for example, when school fees have to be paid before the harvest period. But also unforeseen and sudden money shortfalls can pose serious risks to smallholders' life, for example, in the case of external shocks such as floods or droughts or in case of sickness, when hospital bills have to be paid. Meeting these cash constraints with short-term credits can improve the

---

[12] Agricultural insurance products also imply high risks for an institution, but are mostly outsourced to an insurance company. Additionally, they are mostly still at pilot stage in SSA.
[13] Even though the other MFIs also offer consumption credits, their loan terms are not adapted to the specific features of agriculture and smallholder households and are thus not counted as agricultural loans, and are therefore not very accessible for smallholder farmers.
[14] While livestock is counted as asset finance in most cases, there are some exceptions. If animals or eggs are just bought for fattening or hatching they may count as working capital. Only animals that are used for longer periods, e.g. for milk, wool, or egg production, traction or reproduction activities usually count as assets.

overall profitability of a smallholder household, as they are not forced to sell tangible assets or part of their harvest in advance, mostly at unfavourable prices. (Goodland et al. 1999, 8)

2.2 The history of agricultural finance for smallholder farmers: a change of underlying principles

The current approach of offering financial services to smallholder farmers is heavily influenced by disastrous experiences with agricultural lending programmes during the 1950s and 1960s. While the perception that agricultural lending to smallholder farmers involves high transaction costs and specific risks remained the same, the approach to tackle these risks and costs changed together with the general perception of financial systems and the role of government intervention and subsidies. Table 2 summarizes the main features of the so-called old paradigm of agricultural finance that was prevalent during the 1950s and 1960s and contrasts it with the new paradigm. In the following, these key features of the two paradigms are explained in their respective contexts.

2.2.1 Old paradigm: subsidized agricultural credit

After World War II, worldwide concern about food shortages in development countries led to increased attention to the topic of agricultural development (Gangrade/Chaturvedi 1989, 23, Paddock 1967). High yielding varieties (HYVs) as well as new agricultural technologies such as chemical fertilizers and other agrochemicals were developed and massively promoted to increase global food production.[15] To apply this kind of input intensive agriculture, (smallholder) farmers had to make massive investments. However, they were perceived to be too poor to save and invest their own money or to borrow the money needed for these investments at market interest rates. Therefore, national governments as well as donors felt responsible to intervene and offer the needed money with the hope that the provision of subsidized credits would induce farmers to apply fertilizer, to irrigate, and to adopt HYVs. They founded large state agricultural banks or agricultural credit programmes that received concessionary credits for lending to specific target groups, for example, smallholders wanting to adopt new agricultural technologies, such as

---

[15] This development is known under the term "Green Revolution". There is vast literature on the Green Revolution. An overview can be found in Karim (1986).

new plant varieties, chemical fertilizers, and agro-chemicals. These loans were highly subsidized to keep interest rates low and to accelerate farmers' adoption of the Green Revolution production packages. The heavy subsidies were also thought to compensate the banks for entering into a sector, where they feared high losses due to inherent high transaction costs and risks. In many cases, lending targets were imposed on financial institutions and their performance was evaluated by number of loans issued rather than repayment rates (Table 2). (Nagarajan/Meyer 2005, 3ff.; Klein et al. 1999, 2ff.; Adams/von Pitschke 1992, 1463ff.; Yaron/Benjamin 1997, 41ff.; Meyer 2009, 55ff.)

Table 2: Comparison of paradigms of agricultural finance for smallholder farmers

Feature	Old paradigm: subsidized credits	New paradigm: financial system approach
Main idea	Boost agricultural productivity and reduce poverty through subsidized credit targeted to poor smallholders	Foster rural and agricultural development through the provision of financial services and the reduction of market imperfection and transaction costs
Role of financial markets	Help the poor to adopt new agricultural technologies; stimulate production	Intermediate efficiently: direct resources where they are most efficient
View of users	Borrowers are beneficiaries; they are too poor to save and to pay high (cost covering) interest rates	Clients are borrowers and depositors; they demand various financial services and are able to pay cost-covering interest rates
Source of funds	Governments and donors	Voluntary deposits; refinancing on financial market
Type of institution	State-owned agricultural banks or donor-funded programmes	Commercial MFIs
Role of subsidies	Institutions are heavily subsidy dependent; Subsidies considered necessary to keep interest rates low and reach poor clients	Institutions are increasingly independent of subsidies; Smart subsidies to support institution building and innovations
Viability of institution	Largely ignored	Major concern
Interest rates	Have to be low; interest rate caps	Cost covering interest rates
Evaluation	Number and amount of loans disbursed	Performance (financial viability) and outreach of financial institution
Role of government/donors	Direct intervention in financial systems	Creation of a supporting regulatory framework; support institutional capacity and innovative technologies

Source: based on Charitonenko/Campion 2003, 2.

SSA was mostly bypassed by the introduction of HYVs and other Green Revolution technologies.[16] However, after their independence most African countries were also aware of the importance of smallholder agriculture for development and keen to develop their agricultural sector. Thus, even though the Green Revolution technology was not widely implemented in SSA, SSA countries followed the state-led development paradigm prevalent at this time and state-led agricultural banks, donor-funded agricultural credit programmes, and parastatal marketing boards became widespread in SSA. (IFAD 2003, 5; Jayne et al. 2010, 1393; Kherallah et al. 2000, 8ff.; Adams/von Pitschke 1992, 1463ff.)

In the late 1970s and early 1980s, scientists of the Rural Finance Program at Ohio State University started to heavily criticize government-led banks and subsidized agricultural credit programmes.[17] They argued that the little productivity increase that could be found in some Asian countries was largely offset by the high costs as well as the long-term unsustainability of these subsidized state-led agricultural finance institutions (Binswanger/Khandker 1995, cited after Armendáriz/Morduch 2010, 11). Additionally, the old paradigm did not meet its objectives of income expansion and poverty reduction (Yaron et al. 1997, 3). Since the market rate of interest as a rationing mechanism was lacking, money was often allocated on the basis of social and political concern and not to those with the most worthy projects. Additionally, loans were often badly monitored, because the institutional success was measured by issued credits and not by repayment rates, and many times loans were excused before elections. This led to very high default rates, sometimes up to 95%, an overall borrower perception that credits are given as grants and a general culture of non-repayment. Poor loan recoveries combined with the (politically desired) low interest rates and the non-collection of savings increased the institutions' dependency on subsidies. At the same time, institutions had no incentives to work more efficiently and reach financial sustainability, as long as

---

[16] This had several reasons: first, the sharp increase in oil and fertilizer prices in 1973's oil crisis; secondly, the Green Revolution techniques for rice crops required a good irrigation infrastructure and water management, which was absent in most countries of SSA region; and thirdly, Green Revolution techniques require intensive use and the timely application of inputs and seeds of HYVs which were not within the reach of farmers due to many social and economic factors (IAASTD 2009a, 20).

[17] Ohio State University scientists conducted most of their research in Asian countries and primarily India, because this is where the introduction of HYVs and Green Revolution technologies was most successful. The critique on heavily subsidized state-led agricultural finance can, however, be transferred to SSA countries as well.

money flows were there. (Armendáriz/Morduch 2010, 11; Klein et al. 1999, Yaron/Benjamin 2002, 327; Beck et al. 2011, 121; Nagarajan/Meyer 2005, 3; Klein et al. 1999, 2; Meyer 2009, 55ff.; Meyer 2011, 11)

Under these conditions a permanent credit supply through viable institutions in rural areas could not be established. Some scientists, therefore, even argue that these cheap subsidized credits devastated rural financial markets and thereby even undermined attempts to reduce poverty. (Adams/von Pitschke 1992, 1463; Yaron/Benjamin 1997, 41) As soon as donor funds stopped, most state- or donor-funded agricultural credit programmes imploded due to their unsustainability.

2.2.2 Emergence of a new paradigm

In the years following the 1980s, a number of parallel developments took place: (1) Criticism of the old paradigm grew. (2) MFIs (at this time mostly micro-*credit* institutions) emerged and had some innovative approaches to managing the risks and costs associated with low-income clients. Because of the bad reputation of the state-led model, early MFIs turned to the private sector for inspiration and tried to run their MFIs as businesses and not as a channel for donated money. Their success showed that low-income people can be creditworthy, when using the right lending techniques and are able to pay market-interest rates. (3) The paradigm of privatization and free markets emerged globally. Many SSA countries had to implement structural adjustment programmes (SAPs) and international donors promoted the privatization or dismantling of agricultural marketing parastatals, the deregulation of (agricultural) credit markets, and the elimination of credit and other subsidies. Consequently, most governments and donors stopped their funding, agricultural banks were either closed or privatized, and many agricultural credit programmes imploded as a result. (Adams/von Pitschke 1992, 1466; Dorward et al. 2009, 15; Meyer 2011, 12)

At the same time and influenced by all these changes, a new paradigm called the financial system approach developed and provided a new framework for development finance (Table 2). This more liberal, marked-oriented approach emphasizes the need of functioning financial markets with competitive and financially viable institutions that offer a range of financial services. These services need to be adapted to clients' demands and go beyond the mere provision of credits. Efficient management, market interest rates and the collection of savings should lead to financially viable financial institutions that are independent of the steady flow of donor or government funds. Assessing the performance of these financial institutions according to financial viability[18] and not the number of loans disbursed is, therefore, crucial. The role of governments and donors also changed. They were no longer supposed to channel money through financial institutions or fund them in the long term, but to provide the regulatory framework to support a liberal financial market, help build institutional capacity and support innovations for lowering transaction costs and improving risk management. (Meyer 2011, 12; Zeller 2003, 5; Nagarajan/Meyer 2005, 3ff.) This paradigm was officially taken over into guidelines and approaches of international development organizations in the 1990s (Meyer 2011, 13).[19]

The microfinance industry quickly adopted this new financial system approach, especially the striving for financial sustainability through efficient management and cost covering interest rates, the provision of a broad range of financial products, and the view of their clients as customers and not beneficiaries. In addition to this, the success of MFIs is owed to some more specific innovations connected to their loan products and lending procedures. These allow MFIs to deal with challenges associated with lending to the low-income population, for example: (1) information asymmetry, (2) lack of traditional collateral, and (3) difficulties enforcing contracts and high transaction costs. These new lending technologies coupled with the new paradigm approach led to a substantial spread of microfinance, today known as the microfinance revolution. (Armendáriz/Morduch 2010, 8ff.)

2.2.3 Linking the new paradigm and agricultural finance for smallholder farmers

Under the new financial system paradigm, agricultural finance for smallholder farmers should be provided through the commercial microfinance sector. But even though the microfinance sector grew rapidly over the last decade in SSA, this development largely took place in urban areas and rural centres, where they mostly

---

[18] According to Ledgerwood (1999, 215) "financial viability refers to the ability of an MFI to cover its costs with earned revenues".

[19] Even though the old paradigm has been largely replaced by the new financial system approach, some important remnants remain. According to Helms/Reille (2004; cited in Meyer 2011, 12) "in 2004, nearly 40 countries reported having some form of interest rate ceilings, and several have recently introduced interest rate restrictions [even though] interest rate ceilings can discourage lenders from making small loans with high operation costs". Also "the implicit 'promise' to achieve complete financial self-reliance in short order has been far from fulfilled" (Armendáriz/ Morduch 2011, 24).

serve petty traders and other low-income clients involved in small businesses (Klein et al. 1999, i; Nagarajan/Meyer 2005, 4; Zeller 2003, 3). MFIs were not able to fill the gap that the closure of agricultural development banks left in most countries, thereby leaving rural areas and agriculture underserved (or not served at all) with financial services (FinMark Trust 2011; Beck et al. 2011, 92; Gisbert 2008, 4; Adesina 2010, 74; Morvant-Roux 2008, 5).[20]

There are several reasons for the reluctance of MFIs to provide financial services to smallholder farmers. First, MFIs encounter additional risks and transaction costs in rural areas and agricultural production that they are not familiar with. Their lending technologies developed for low-income clients cannot be transferred as is to the agricultural smallholder sector; they have to be adapted first. Many MFIs lack the knowledge of how to adapt their lending technologies and procedures and/or fear the initial costs. Secondly, the striving for financial sustainability implies setting interest rates that cover the risks and costs of lending to a specific group. Consequently, loans for smallholder farmers would have higher interest rates to cover the additional risks and transaction costs. While strong supporters of the new paradigm implicitly acknowledge that smallholders are able to pay high interest rates, some authors raise their doubts.[21] They question whether or not agricultural activities generate enough revenues to pay high interest rates (Brandt 2004, 48; Harper 2008; Morvant-Roux 2008, 15; Temu 2009, 5; Meyer 2011, 21). Both issues, that is, the adaption of microfinance lending technologies to agricultural finance of smallholder farmers as well as the questions surrounding interest rates will be addressed in Chapter 7.

---

[20] Due to a lack of data, a more comprehensive picture of the state of agricultural finance in SSA cannot be drawn.

[21] As far as the author knows, there is no open discussion on the adequate level of interest rate levels for smallholder farmers in literature. Supporters of the new paradigm strongly reject subsidies and promote cost covering interest rates for all clients (including smallholders) (Armendáriz/Morduch 2010, 332; Klein et al. 1999, 3ff.; Zeller 2003, 5). Other authors as well as a range of development practitioners raise their doubt about this.

3 Risks and costs of agricultural lending for smallholder farmers

Every finance institution faces a variety of risks and costs. Within the microfinance sector, risks and costs are enhanced by the fact that individuals of the low-income population require smaller loan amounts and do not have traditional collateral for their borrowed money. MFIs therefore have to find mechanisms to handle the relatively higher transaction costs associated with small loan amounts and assure the repayment in the absence of traditional collateral. In addition to these costs and risks, lending to smallholder farmers implies additional agriculture-related risks as well as specific challenges and transaction costs associated with remote rural areas.

3.1 (Credit) risks specific to agricultural lending for smallholder farmers

Table 3 illustrates the most common risks a (micro-) finance institution has to manage.

Table 3: Micro-finance risk categories

FINANCIAL RISK	
Credit or loan default risk	**Funding/Refinancing risks**
• Asymmetric information, adverse selection and moral hazard • Lack of traditional collateral • Market and price risk • External risk • Risks related to loan product design • Client risk	• Liquidity risk • Interest rate risk • Foreign exchange/currency risk

STRATEGIC RISK	OPERATIONAL RISKS
Risks related to weak governance and leadership, poor strategic decisions or to regulatory and administrative reasons	*Risks emanating from a failure of internal systems, processes, technology, and humans*
<ul><li>External regulations and laws</li><li>Competition</li><li>External and internal governance</li><li>Relationship with governments and donors</li></ul>	<ul><li>Transaction</li><li>Fraud and integrity</li><li>Technology</li><li>**Human resources**</li><li>Legal and compliance</li></ul>
Features marked in bold represents aspects where specific challenges occur once an MFI starts to provide agricultural finance to smallholder farmers.	

Source: own illustration adapted from Goldberg/Palladini 2010, 4 and Klein et al. 1999, 13ff.

Table 3 organizes risks in three categories: financial, strategic, and operational risks.[22] All of these risks can threaten the well-being of a financial institution. The risks marked in bold are the ones where specific challenges occur once an MFI starts to do provide agricultural finance to smallholder farmers. Table 3 shows that additional risks due to lending to smallholders are concentrated under credit risks. Even though **human resources** are listed under operational risks, there is a close link to credit risk when it comes to agricultural finance for smallholder farmers. Without having qualified staff that can apply their thorough understanding of agriculture during loan design, credit assessment, and monitoring, credit risks are largely increased.

Liquidity risk is not a credit risk but is rather associated with the refinancing capacities of an MFI. It occurs when a bank is not able to meet its cash requirements (Klein et al. 1999, 13). Agricultural lending implies high liquidity risks due to the seasonality of agriculture and thus smallholder households' cash flows. Due to the synchronic timing of agricultural activities in a given area, all smallholders have cash surpluses and an increased savings capacity at the same time after harvest, but also demand working capital loans at the same time before planting. External effects (e.g. weather extremes) can also create liquidity risks, because they typically affect all smallholders in a particular area at the same time, thus creating a high covariant risk. To mitigate these liquidity risks, lenders need to have large cash reserves to meet depositors' withdrawals at times when a whole group of bor-

---

[22] Different authors organize risks differently, depending on their way of understanding risks. The present table is, therefore, only one possible way of structuring risks for financial institutions.

rowers cannot repay, which is especially challenging for small MFIs. (Christen/Pearce 2005, 4; Klein et al. 1999, 14; Meyer 2011, 9; Zeller 2003, 17)

Credit risk refers to "borrowers who are unable or unwilling to repay the loan principle and to service the interest rate charges" (Klein et al. 1999, 13). This risk can be enhanced through several factors: asymmetric information, adverse selection, moral hazard, lack of traditional collateral, market and price risk, external risks, poor loan product design as well as specific client risk. While asymmetric information, adverse selection, moral hazard and collateral limitations are the same for traditional microfinance and agricultural finance for smallholder farmers, the other credit risks are specific for the latter.

Asymmetric information, adverse selection, moral hazard, and lack of collateral
Before proceeding to the specific risks of lending to smallholder farmers, it is helpful to understand the general role of information and collateral in credit markets and the risks associated with a lack of these two.

Every credit market is characterized by *asymmetric information*: borrowers know more about their creditworthiness and risk-taking behaviour than financial institutions. Asymmetric information can lead to two difficulties, adverse client selection, and moral hazard difficulties. *Adverse selection* describes a situation where the financial institutions cannot adequately distinguish safer from riskier borrowers due to asymmetric information. It is therefore difficult to reject too risky clients or charge riskier clients higher interest rates to compensate for their greater risk of default. When the same average interest rate is charged to all borrowers, safer borrowers cross-subsidize riskier borrowers or—if average interest rates are set too high—safer borrowers refuse to borrow at all and leave the bank with riskier than average customers.[23] Having a large number of riskier than average borrowers enhances the credit risk and can lead to a decline of the overall portfolio quality. (Armendáriz/Morduch 2010, 39ff.; Goldberg/Palladini 2010, 5)

Moral hazard refers to a situation where the borrower decides not to repay a loan or not to put all of his/her effort into the financed project, because s/he does not expect negative consequences (e.g. legal actions taken by the financial institution). Due to asymmetric information, a financial institution does not know whether a client willingly defaulted or whether or not sufficient efforts were put into the fi-

---

[23] Riskier projects often have a higher return on investments if the project succeeds and, therefore, riskier clients are more willing to pay higher interest rates, especially if the likelihood of losing collateral or being prosecuted when the project fails is low.

40 Risks and costs of agricultural lending for smallholder farmers

nanced project unless the financial institution is heavily involved in monitoring, which in itself is very costly. (Armendáriz/Morduch 2010, 48ff., 58; Meyer 2011, 8)[24] The old paradigm of agricultural finance, under which loan repayments were often not enforced, people received government funding under the guise of "loans" or loans were politically excused, created a distorted credit culture (Klein et al. 1999, 16). In many countries in SSA, the smallholder is therefore a "well-trained defaulter" (Braun 2004, 48) and does not anticipate negative consequences from not repaying a loan.

In well-functioning, traditional credit markets, adverse selection and moral hazard are addressed by having effective ways to gather and evaluate client information (e.g. credit-reporting agencies, credit history) and by taking marketable assets as collateral, which can be pledged and enforced in case of default. Easily accessible information, such as a credit history, business records, or a bank account with regular cash flows, is typically not available in the context of microfinance and smallholder finance. Additionally, smallholder farmers have severe *loan collateral limitations*. Land is normally widely accepted as collateral by financial institutions, because it is fixed and not easily destroyed. However, even if smallholder farmers own their land (and not only lease it), they often cannot prove the legal ownership over this land, because formal land titles and clear property rights do not exist in many SSA countries (Temu 2009, 5). And even if clear property rights exist, there are difficulties in seizing land of the poor. First, contract enforcement is in itself challenging in many SSA countries. Often traditional law does not allow seizing land and the judicial system, especially in rural areas, is not able to enforce laws against this background (Brandt 2004, 48). Secondly, seizing land of poor smallholders would, in most cases, endanger the livelihood of a whole family. This does not only run against the social mission of most MFIs, but the MFI would probably also run into stiff community opposition. Furthermore, moveable assets, such as livestock and agricultural equipment, cannot easily serve as collateral, as smallholders must provide a proof of purchase and ideally have insurance coverage on them, which is rarely the case. (Klein et al. 1999, 15)

So the success of MFIs is based on their alternative loan procedures and mechanisms that compensate for borrowers' lack of traditional collateral as well as

---

[24] A thorough explanation of moral hazard and adverse selection can be found in Armendáriz/Morduch 2010, 39ff.

information asymmetries.[25] However, as will be seen in Chapter 4, not all of these techniques are suitable for agricultural lending to smallholder farmers.

External risks: production and yield risks
External risks refer to risks that are beyond human control, such as disease, death, or natural disaster. They are hardly controllable by MFIs and pose severe risks to loan repayment. While most MFIs try to mitigate the risk of, for example, death of a borrower by attaching a compulsory insurance to the loan, external agricultural risks cannot yet be mitigated through insurances in SSA.[26] Weather extremes, pests, and diseases are among the biggest external agricultural risks in lending to smallholders, because they can hardly be controlled. Extreme weather events, like severe droughts or heavy floods, can destroy an entire yield and thereby a whole year's work. But also minor weather events like irregular rains (either late rains or rains during harvest time) as well as pests and other plant diseases can severely affect yields. (Christen/Pearce 2005, 4; Meyer 2011, 9; Zeller 2003, 17) These risks specifically impact smallholders wanting to generate a higher income at the price of concentrated risk, for example, concentrating their production on a high-input cash crop (Klein et al. 1999, 14).

Market and price risks
Weak input and output markets as well as volatile prices also increase the risk of default. In many countries of SSA, agricultural input and output markets are imperfect and communication and information structures are lacking. Agricultural prices, and therefore smallholders' incomes, fluctuate heavily and are hardly predictable, because they are a function of the actual (national and worldwide) supply at the time of harvest, which in turn depends on local and global weather and market variations. A lack of storage possibilities, for example, warehouses, adds to the problem, because smallholders often have to sell their crop at a low price during the harvest season and cannot wait until prices rise again. This leads to two major problems for MFIs. First, agricultural production often has low returns, which increases the default risk. Secondly, there is a relatively long period between the decision to plant a crop or start a livestock business and the actual realization of farm output. Market prices, and thus business return, are unknown at the time a loan is granted

---

[25] The best-known mechanism is probably group lending. There are, however, a range of other mechanisms, which will be explained in Chapter 4.
[26] Some pilots on weather index insurance exist, but not yet on a large scale (see Chapter 7).

and it is therefore difficult to calculate the debt capacity of a borrower. This problem is even more severe for perennial tree crops. (Christen/Pearce 2005, 2ff.; Klein et al. 1999, 15; Zeller 2003, 17)

Risk related to loan product design
Inadequate loan product design (e.g. loan amount, repayment schedule, etc.) can create additional credit risk (Goldberg/Palladini 2010, 6). All loans that are mainly repaid through agricultural activities need to be adapted to the agricultural life cycle (either crop or animal life cycle), which is typically characterized by a delay between the investment and the first return. In most cases, the return also comes in one lump sum after harvest. The typical microfinance loans with regular, (often weekly) repayments starting soon after loan disbursement would, therefore, lead to repayment difficulties for smallholders.[27] Additionally, agricultural production is very sensitive to timely planting, fertilization, weeding, application of phytosanitary measures, and harvesting, which may change from year to year according to weather conditions. To be used for their intended purposes, agricultural loans must be disbursed in a timely manner; otherwise the activity for which the loan was granted (e.g. planting) may already be over. MFIs, therefore, require thorough knowledge of the respective life cycle of the plant/animal they grant loans for, as well as current weather data and close monitoring of the agricultural situation in their respective areas to manage the credit risk. (BMZ 2005, 17; Christen/Pearce 2005, 3; Klein et al. 1999, 12ff.; Temu 2009, 5; Zeller 2003, 14)

Client risk
Literature mentions several additional constraints in rural areas and agricultural lending that also increase credit risks. These include higher incidences of poverty among smallholders, low education and financial literacy levels, low agricultural productivity, and greater difficulties in dealing with illness, accidents and other life cycle risks. (BMZ 2005, 17; Brandt 2004, 48; Meyer 2011, 9; Zeller 2003, 14)

3.2 Costs specific to agricultural lending for smallholder farmers

Higher costs of microfinance stem from the fact that transaction costs of financial services generally have a large fixed cost component, making unit costs for smaller saving deposits or smaller loans high compared to larger financial transactions, ir-

---

[27] This topic will be further elaborated in Chapter 4.

respective of the lending technology used (Zeller 2003, 10). On top of this, agricultural finance for smallholder farmers has the following features, which lead to higher transaction costs.

Dispersed clients and bad infrastructure
Smallholder households are often located in sparsely populated areas with poor communication and transport infrastructures. Distances from MFI branches to smallholder farmers are long and poor rural transportation facilities in many countries increase the costs of loan appraisal and monitoring. Smallholder farmers also face high transaction costs due to the opportunity costs of lost working time in case of travelling to the MFI for signing the loan contract, withdrawing (loan) money, and making repayments. (Klein et al. 1999, 11; Temu 2009, 3; Zeller 2003, 14)

Seasonality
The seasonality of agriculture also has important implications for MFIs' transaction costs. Compared to traditional microfinance loans, credits for agricultural production are usually required for longer periods and repaid in one or two lump sums. Repayment capacity and willingness, therefore, cannot be monitored by frequent repayment installments (as is the case in traditional microfinance) but require more costly approaches (e.g. regular farm visits). The uneven distribution of agricultural lending activities over the year may also lead to increased fixed costs of personal. (Klein et al. 1999, 11ff.)

Heterogeneity of smallholder households and time sensitivity of agriculture
The diversified household income of most smallholder households as well as the time sensitivity of agricultural activities requires good and regularly updated agricultural knowledge along with the ability to assess the overall cash flow of a farm household. Compared to urban lending, more information is probably needed, which requires more time (and expenses) during loan assessment. Additionally, loan officers need a wider range of qualifications, covering finance as well as agricultural knowledge. This either increases salaries or the costs of staff training. (Klein et al. 1999, 13)

4 Traditional microfinance risk and cost management approaches: do they work for smallholder farmers?

The microfinance industry successfully developed instruments and approaches to tackle the credit risk of low-income borrowers without traditional collateral and/or proper business records. Through specific loan product features, instruments and procedures during loan assessment and monitoring, MFIs manage to address the adverse selection and moral hazard risks, which are closely related to collateral limitations and asymmetric information as described in Chapter 3. High transaction costs associated with lending small amounts to low-income clients are tackled by high volumes per loan officer and with highly standardized lending procedures that allow cutting down on loan assessment and monitoring costs. Additionally, traditional microfinance follows the new financial paradigm and thus tries to establish financially viable institutions implying cost covering interest rates.

Studies on agricultural finance and microfinance indicate that loan features and lending procedures of traditional microfinance products are often unsuitable or unattractive for smallholder farmers (Christen/Pearce 2005, 33; Harper 2005; Matovu 2009, 105).

A horizontal study conducted by Jessop et al. (2012) based on country research in six countries,[28] for example, concluded that

> "Often, financial institutions lack financial service products that take into account the specificity of agriculture (...). Thus, they present farmers with credit repayment proposals that do not match the reality of farming. (...) They [also] expect information and offer tailor-made services that are not in accordance with the information opacity of smallholders (...)." (Jessop et al. 2012, 27)

The following paragraphs present key traditional microfinance loan product features as well as instruments and procedures used for risk and cost management of traditional MFIs and discusses whether these are working for smallholder farmers or not. All of them will be taken up in Chapter 7, where findings from the interviews suggest how these features and procedures can be adapted to better suit smallholder farmers.

---

[28] Cambodia, Mali, Senegal, Tanzania, Thailand, Tunisia.

4.1 Loan product design for risk mitigation in traditional microfinance

Table 4 depicts typical features of traditional microfinance credits.

Table 4: Typical loan features of traditional microfinance credits

Loan product feature	Characteristics of traditional microfinance loans
Loan amount	Small
Interest rate	Cost covering, often high
Loan term	Short
Repayment frequency	Regular small amounts (often weekly or bi-monthly)
Collateral requirements	Joint liability groups; non-traditional collateral
Additional features	Target women

Source: own illustration.

Loan amount

Loan amounts of traditional MFIs typically have a small size, which reflects the relatively low debt capacity of low-income clients. Many MFIs also restrict the loan size for first-time borrowers and increase it with each loan to reduce the MFI's risk and create the incentive for the clients to repay their loan through the promise of a higher loan in the future (Ledgerwood 1999, 134). Loan amount size is, however, not set, but agreed on based on the debt capacity of the borrower. It is thus a feature that is compatible with agricultural finance for smallholder farmers.

Interest rates

Effective interest rates (EIRs)[29] for microcredit are low relative to private moneylenders but are mostly high compared to rates for larger loans from private CBs (Meyer 2011, 21). The higher costs stem from the relatively higher transaction costs of small credits as well as the higher risk associated with uncollateralized microcredit. Transaction costs for small loans are relatively higher, because costs for meeting the client for loan appraisal, processing the loan disbursement, and loan monitoring remain more or less the same irrespectively of the loan size. Thus, smaller loans are comparatively more expensive than bigger loans. (Meyer 2011, 14ff.)

---

[29] Effective interest rates refer to the inclusion of all direct financial costs of a loan into one interest rate.
They incorporate interest, fees, charges, interest calculation method (flat or reducing), and other loan requirements into the financial costs of a loan. (Ledgerwood 1999, 143)

To get a rough impression of average interest rates charged by MFIs, one can refer to the median yield on gross portfolio (Meyer 2011, 21; Armendáriz/Morduch 2010, 247).[30] Between 2009 and 2011 the median yield on gross portfolio (adjusted for inflation) for operational self-sufficient (OSS) MFIs[31] from all over the world represented in MIX market[32] was between 17% and 22%. It was higher for African MFIs, where it ranged between 21% and 26% for OSS MFIs and went up to 28% for small OSS African MFIs (see Annex B for detailed figures).

Assuming that MFIs have to include the higher risks and transaction costs of lending to smallholder farmers as described in Chapter 3 into their interest rate calculations, one can assume that interest rates for agricultural loans for smallholder farmers would even be higher than this. Whether or not smallholders are able to pay these high cost covering interest rates remains an open question in literature. Although this should be a central issue in the discussion about smallholder finance, because "if the interest rates are higher than their client's returns, the long-term impact will be to impoverish and not to enrich them" (Harper 2008, 87), there is hardly any empirical evidence concerning the question of "adequate" interest rate levels for smallholders. While strong supporters of the new paradigm implicitly acknowledge that smallholders are able to pay high interest rates, some authors raise their doubts.[33] They question whether or not agriculture is productive and profitable enough to warrant high (commercial) interest rates and also consider the additional risks and higher transaction costs of small loans for farmers (Jessop et al. 2012, 82ff.; Brandt 2004, 48; Harper 2008; Morvant-Roux 2008, 15; Temu 2009, 5; Meyer 2011, 21). So far, comparatively little research has been conducted in recent years on rates of return of agricultural production relative to interest rates (Meyer 2011, 21). Meyer (2011, 21) presents some empirical studies that point to the possibility of earning enough returns through agriculture to cover high interest rates.

---

[30] Portfolio yield is calculated by dividing the interest and fee income during a respective period by the average outstanding loan portfolio of the same period and thus indicates how much an MFI received in payments from its clients during the period (Arunachalam 2006, 1; Armendáriz/Morduch 2010, 247).
[31] Operational Self-Sufficiency (OSS) is calculated as follows: Financial Revenue/(Financial Expense + Impairment Loss + Operating Expense).
[32] MIX market (www.mixmarket.org) is a data hub where MFIs and supporting institutions share institutional data to broaden transparency and market insight. The platform is provided by MIX, a non-profit organization headquartered in Washington, DC (Mixmarket 2014).
[33] The impression of their implicit acknowledgment derives from their strong rejection of subsidies in general, and interest rate subsidies or interest rate caps in particular.

Compared to microenterprises, rates of return are, however, much lower (Meyer 2011, 22ff.; Harper 2008, 90ff.).[34]

This controversial issue of interest rates will further be discussed in Section 7.1.2 based on the information from the conducted interviews.

Loan term and repayment frequency

The loan term, that is, the period of time during which the entire loan must be repaid,

> "is one of the most important variables in microfinance, [because it] affects the repayment schedule, the revenue to the MFI, the financing costs for the client, and the ultimate suitability of the use of the loan. (...) The closer an organization matches loan terms to its client's needs, the easier it is for the client to 'carry' the loan and the more likely that payments will be made on time and in full." (Ledgerwood 1999, 134)

Microfinance loan terms are mostly short, that is, under 1 year, and are in many cases combined with frequent repayment installments starting soon after the initial disbursement of the loan. The frequency of the installments is often weekly or bi-monthly, sometimes also monthly and is often combined with a group meeting. There are several ways in which these frequent repayments help minimize the MFIs' credit risk. First, they serve as indicator for the well-being of the client's business (if s/he is able to repay, the business is running well). Secondly, they are considered essential to maintain the financial discipline of the client in the absence of physical collateral. Thirdly, frequent repayments attract borrowers with regular income streams besides the funded project (otherwise they could not repay the early installments). This reduces the MFI's risk as these clients will be able to repay the loan with the alternative income stream in case their investment fails. And fourthly, frequent repayments allow the MFI to reuse the money faster for other clients, thereby making the lending business for the MFI more profitable. (Armendáriz/Morduch 2010, 148ff.; Meyer 2011, 14ff.; Ledgerwood 1999, 135; Dorward et al. 2009, 12)

Short loan terms with frequent repayments can present difficulties for smallholder farmers.

---

[34] Harper (2008, 98ff.) refers to a study of about 215 microenterprises that produced an average annual return of 847%. He compares it to some data on rates of return for farm investment, which are between 25% and 160% and, in most cases, below 100%.

While loans with loan terms of up to 1 year can be used for purchasing agricultural working capital for annual crops and some livestock activities that generate revenues within 1 year, perennial crops (e.g. coffee, cocoa) and bigger assets cannot be financed through short-term microcredit. Frequent repayment installments even pose a higher loan default risk on smallholders, even if their household income is diversified and they have some (regular) off-farm income. Due to the seasonal nature of agriculture, smallholders earn the main part of their income in one lump sum after harvest. Therefore, regular repayments of the loan principle cannot be met by most smallholder farmers. They would thus default on some of their loan repayment, even if their agricultural revenue were high enough to repay the loan after harvest. Figure 2 illustrates the effect of different loan terms and repayment frequencies on the household cash situation of a fictive smallholder household with a monthly off-farm income of USD 40 and an annual farm income of USD 1,000 arising from crop cultivation. It is further assumed that the smallholder needs a loan for agricultural inputs of USD 400 at the beginning of the agricultural season and the crop can be harvested and sold after 8 months, leading to an income of USD 1,000.

Figure 2: Effects of different loan terms and repayment schedules

Scenario 1: 8-month loan term, 24% annual interest on declining balance; frequent repayments

Period	Household (Hh) income	Loan	Hh net income
0		(−400)	
1	40	58	−18
2	40	57	−17
3	40	56	−16
4	40	55	−15
5	40	54	−14
6	40	53	−13
7	40	52	−12
8	1,040	51	989.00
Total	1,320	436	884.00

Scenario 3: 8-month loan term; 24% annual interest on declining balance; frequent interest repayment and single end term principle payment

Period	Hh income	Loan	Hh net income
0		(−400)	
1	40	8	32
2	40	8	32
3	40	8	32
4	40	8	32
5	40	8	32
6	40	8	32
7	40	8	32
8	1,040	408	632
Total	1,320	464	856

Scenario 2: 12-month loan term; 24% annual interest on declining balance; frequent repayments

Period	Hh income	Loan	Hh net income
0		(−400)	
1	40	41.33	−1.33
2	40	40.66	−0.66
3	40	40	0
4	40	39.33	0.67
5	40	38.66	1.34
6	40	38	2
7	40	37.33	2.67
8	1,040	36.66	1,003.34
9	40	36	4
10	40	35.33	4.67
11	40	34.66	5.34
12	40	34	6
Total	1,480	452	1,028

Overall scenario:
Smallholder farmer with a monthly off-farm income of USD 40 and an annual farm income of USD 1,000 from crop cultivation. A loan of USD 400 is needed for agricultural inputs and the crop can be harvested and sold after 8 months, leading to an income of USD 1,000.

Source: own figure based on Ledgerwood 1999, 134ff.; calculated with MicroFinance Transparency (2012).

Scenarios 1 and 2 depict the net income situation of a smallholder, who has to meet monthly repayments for a loan of USD 400 at different loan terms. In Scenario 1, the loan term corresponds to the agricultural activity of the smallholder, but the farmer has to meet regular repayments. One can see that s/he is in default for the entire loan period and can only repay the loan after the cash from selling the crop comes in. Scenario 2 represents a situation, where neither the loan term nor the repayment frequency is adapted to the agricultural activity. Even though the smallholder is probably able to repay the loan installments after harvest (9–12 months) with the cash income derived from the agricultural activity, the MFI faces the risk that the smallholder will have already spent the harvest income on something else. Scenario 3 shows the situation, in which the loan term as well as the repayment schedule is adapted to the smallholder's agricultural activity. S/he repays the interest monthly and the loan principle in one lump payment after selling the crop. Even though the total cost of the loan is the highest in this scenario at USD 64 compared to USD 36 in Scenario 1, s/he is able to meet all loan installments without defaulting and without having a negative household income for several months. This example shows that the defaulting risk is greatly enhanced with unadapted loan products and that the typical microfinance loan term and repayment schedule would lead to default for the smallholder even if s/he was eligible under different terms.

Collateral requirements
In many cases, joint liability group lending, under which individuals secure their fellow group members, serves as a substitute for collateral. Since groups also fulfil a range of other purposes during loan assessment and monitoring, the group lending mechanism is explained in the next section. In addition to joint group liability, some MFIs also require some additional non-traditional collateral, such as livestock, household items, or housing. Rather than having a high resale value, the personal value is of importance in serving as collateral. In case of default, the MFI does not have to take possession of the collateral, but only needs to deny access to the collateral to encourage repayment. Some MFIs also require (regular) upfront savings as cash collateral or the co-signing of the loan by personal guarantors. (Armendáriz/Morduch 2010, 155; Klein et al. 1999, 19) Generally, the use of non-traditional collateral is also applicable to smallholders. Only regular upfront savings can pose a problem to smallholder with rather cyclical and bulky cash incomes.

Additional loan features
Many MFIs focus on women, as they seem to be more reliable when it comes to repaying their loans (Armendáriz/Morduch 2010, 158). According to the Microcredit Summit Campaign (Daley-Harris 2009, cited after Armendáriz/Morduch 2010, 211), at the end of 2007 around 70% of all microfinance clients worldwide were women. This tendency can restrict agricultural finance for smallholder farmers as most cash crop farming is done by men (Meyer 2011, 16).

4.2 Loan assessment and monitoring for risk mitigation in traditional microfinance

Different instruments are used to assess the creditworthiness of clients (before issuing the loan) and to enforce repayments (after the loan was issued) during loan assessment and loan monitoring. A client's ability and willingness to repay can be analysed by looking at the five Cs: character, capacity, capital, collateral, and (market) conditions. If any of these components is poorly analysed, the credit risk will increase (Churchill/Coster 2001, 38ff.).

Table 5 depicts the five Cs and the instruments with which they can be assessed during the loan appraisal. It also shows different instruments that can be used as repayment incentives. One can see that joint liability group lending plays a big role in microfinance, since it can be used to analyse different client characteristics and serves as a repayment incentive at the same time. The illustrated instruments will be explained after a short description of the five Cs.

Table 5: Credit risk mitigation during loan assessment and monitoring in traditional microfinance

Feature	Instrument
Loan assessment	
Character	• Group lending • Interview family, friends, opinion leader in community • Visit household and business
Capacity to repay	• Assess business plan • Assess household cash flow: good to have diversified household income and business experience
Capital	(Assets and liabilities)
Collateral	• Collateral substitutes: joint liability group guarantee; personal guarantor, cash collateral • Non-traditional collateral
(Market) conditions	• Business experience of borrower
Loan monitoring	
Repayment incentives	• Group lending: social pressure, staggered loan disbursements, group repayments • Dynamic incentives: threatening to stop lending, progressive lending • Frequent repayment installments • Public repayments

Source: own illustration based on Churchill/Coster (2001, 38ff.).

(1) In microfinance, *character* is the most important trait when selecting a new borrower, as many potential borrowers have no record to demonstrate their capacity to

repay or any traditional collateral to ensure their loan. Having a "good" character means being willing to repay the loan even if the business fails. Character can be assessed by the loan officer through interviews with the potential borrower, his/her neighbours, community leaders, etc. or by using peer groups (group lending). (2) *Capacity* refers to whether a client's cash flow can service the interest and loan repayments. Because the lines between the (potential) business and the household's cash flow are often blurred and due to the fungibility of money,[35] loan officers often try to look at the cash flow of the whole household and/or try to assess the capacity to repay without taking into account the effect of the loan on the business. (3) Some MFIs also try to assess the *capital* of a business, that is, its assets and liabilities. This feature is, however, more important with higher loan amounts and, therefore, not further elaborated on in this paper. (4) As microfinance is developed for people without traditional *collateral*, collateral refers here to mechanisms that can serve as collateral substitutes (joint liability group lending, restrictive product terms, and compulsory savings) or to non-traditional collateral as described in Section 4.1. The type of collateral thereby is not as important as the personal value the client attaches to it. In most cases, it is not cost-effective to liquidate the collateral if a borrower cannot repay the loan. Collateral is, therefore, more an indication of the applicant's commitment during loan assessment. (5) *(Market) conditions* are often hard to assess for MFIs, because loan officers usually do not have the expertise to analyse the market conditions for all kinds of businesses. A usual requirement is, therefore, that the applicant is already in the business for a certain amount of time and thus knows the market and market risks, before s/he can apply for a loan. (Churchill/Coster 2001, 38ff.)

In agricultural lending for smallholder farmers, the five Cs are also assessed through most of the instruments listed in Table 5. However, some of the instruments have certain restrictions or follow a different logic when lending to smallholder farmers. These will be explained in the following paragraphs. Additionally, the interviewed MFIs added some instruments and procedures when lending to smallholder farmers. These will be described in Chapter7.

Group lending is probably the best-known microfinance instrument. It refers to an arrangement where a group of individuals without collateral form a group to obtain loans from a lender (Armendáriz/Morduch 2010, 97ff.). In many cases, it is

---

[35] Fungibility of money refers to the fact that an MFI cannot control whether a client uses the loan money for the stated investment or for other purposes.

54   Traditional microfinance risk and cost management approaches

combined with a joint group liability that serves as collateral substitute for a group loan or for group members' individual loans. Thus, if one member faces difficulties in repaying the loan, the others have to pay on his/her behalf.[36]

Group lending with a joint liability contract can mitigate the adverse selection and moral hazard risk that is enhanced through asymmetric information and a lack of collateral as described in Section 3.1. Besides being a collateral substitute, joint liability also encourages the group to use their internal information to carefully decide who is a credible credit risk and will be admitted into their group, since the whole group bears the negative consequences of a defaulting member (repaying the loan or being denied future loans). Once credits are disbursed, group members have incentives to monitor each other's projects as well as to inflict penalties upon group members that take excessive risks. They will also help enforce loan repayment to avoid having to repay for their fellow group members. This not only substantially reduces the lender's costs of screening and monitoring loans and enforcing debt repayments, but also mitigates the moral hazard inefficiencies that are normally caused by the difficulty of monitoring and controlling the borrower's behaviour after the loan disbursement. (Armendáriz/Morduch 2010, 108ff.; Ledgerwood 1999, 70; Meyer 2011, 14) To systemically introduce the loan monitoring and enforcement role of groups, some banks stagger their loan disbursement. This means that not all people of the group receive their loan disbursement at the same time, but only after others successfully repaid part of their loan (Armendáriz/Morduch 2010, 100).[37]

---

[36] A range of different group lending arrangements exist. Different MFIs prefer different group sizes, group members can receive individual loans or one single group loan that they split among themselves, and the existence of a group guarantee is not always compulsory. Some MFIs, among them Grameen Bank, only continued to use joint liability for very small loans and new clients but dropped it for clients with some credit history as joint liability lending has some drawbacks, e.g. being less flexible. They continued group meeting, however, to reduce their transaction costs. A thorough explanation of different group lending mechanisms can be found in Armendáriz/Morduch (2010, 97ff.).

[37] Grameen Bank developed a system where two group members receive their loan first. If they repay all their installments in time, the second two members receive their loan after 4–6 weeks. The chairperson's loan is only disbursed after another 4–6 weeks if all other members meet all their installments. This is known as 2:2:1 staggering (Armendáriz/Morduch 2010, 100). It is important to note that loan staggering is not an inherent mechanism of group lending, but can be added to improve the monitoring and repayment enforcement role of the group.

Even without joint liability, meeting borrowers in groups has some advantages. Meeting borrowers in groups rather than individually greatly reduces transaction costs for the MFI. Regular group meeting with the attendance of a loan officer can be used by the MFI to keep up to date with the newest developments in the smallholder community and any problems can be resolved on the spot. (Armendáriz/Morduch 2010, 98).

As will be seen in Chapter 7, group lending can be applied to the smallholder sector. However, some features of rural areas and the agricultural sector can limit the risk mitigation role of groups. First, in sparsely populated rural areas with a poor infrastructure, travelling costs and the expended time of a loan officer can be dramatically reduced through meeting borrowers in groups. The costs are, however, transferred to the smallholders. Attending regular meetings can be very time consuming and implies high travelling costs for farmers. Additionally smallholders may lack information about each other when living in remote areas, and peer monitoring costs can be high and social punishment for non-compliance difficult to implement. (Armendáriz/Morduch 2010, 138) Secondly, in small villages and among close friends, strong social bonds can subvert the risk mitigation goal of groups. These strong social ties might not allow selecting group members due to their risk profile, but rather based on social bonds, kinship, or other characteristics. Social ties in combination with distorted credit cultures (see Section 2.2) can also lead to higher incidences of negative solidarity, which is the case when a whole group chooses to default. (Armendáriz/Morduch 2010, 123) Thirdly, the use of staggered loan disbursements as a mean of enforcing mutual monitoring and loan repayment is not transferrable to smallholder crop farmers. Due to the time sensitivity of farming, all smallholders in a certain region start their agricultural season around the same time and, therefore, also need their loan disbursement at the same time. It makes thus no sense to receive a fertilizer loan 4 weeks after the fertilizer needs to be applied, only because one belongs to the part of the group receiving the loan later. Fourthly, group lending offers less flexibility, as all group members generally have the same loan term, the same repayment schedule and are punished in case one of their fellow group members defaults. This can be difficult in circumstances where farmers require loans for crops with different growing cycles or where external events are the cause for individual default. Fifthly, joint liability can mitigate the risk of intentional default by smallholder farmers and/or of smallholders that cannot repay, because they did not apply good agricultural practices. It has its limitations, however, in mitigating loan defaults due to external events that negatively impact the revenues of all farmers in a given area, such as weather extremes or pest and diseases.

Although group lending is one of the best-known instruments of risk mitigation in microfinance, "today, group lending is just one element that makes microfinance different from conventional banking" (Armendáriz/Morduch 2010, 137). There are further mechanisms and instruments used by MFIs to gain information and ensure repayments. They can be used in combination with group lending as well as with individual lending approaches and "institutions are increasingly finding that they can pick and choose different elements" (Armendáriz/Morduch 2010, 137).

Interviewing family, friends, neighbours, and community leaders and visit the borrower's household and business to assess the prospective borrowers' character as well as the trustworthiness of the information s/he provides is another important way to tackle the asymmetric information challenge. This implies that loan officers do not stay in their branches analysing the business documents of a prospective client, but visit their client's houses, families, and businesses (Armendáriz/Morduch 2010, 160; Churchill/Coster 2001, 39; Klein et al. 1999, 30).When lending to smallholder farmers, this kind of information gathering can imply higher transaction costs for loan officers due to the poor infrastructure and costly transportation. Additionally, loan officers need to be willing to wear gumboots, walk around fields, and be able to estimate field sizes and assess the use of good agricultural practices just by looking at a field to verify the potential borrowers' information. Recruiting loan officers with these qualifications or training loan officers in these techniques might imply higher costs for an MFI.

During these "field visits" loan officers also try to *assess the borrower's business plan as well as the whole family household income and cash flow*, instead of just assessing the income from the prospective business. As micro-clients often have diversified income-generating activities to mitigate their own household risk, MFIs cannot be sure that the money they lend is used for the intended purpose. Assessing all household activities can thus give a better picture of the risk level of a household. (Dorward et al. 2009, 11; Churchill/Coster 2001, 40) Some MFIs even calculate the repayment capacity of a borrower without taking into account the expected revenue from the loan in question. In that way, a loan can be repaid even if the prospective business is not successful. (Armendáriz/Morduch 2010, 150; Harper 2005, 3) As will be seen in Chapter 7, assessing the whole household income of smallholders as well as their agricultural business plan (what do they want to plant at which costs and at what expected returns) is also important in lending to smallholder farmers. It is, however, more complex (and thus more expensive) to analyse the prospective agricultural income. This is due to highly fluctuating market prices for agriculture and also due to the alternative opportunities for using some of the produced agricultural products. Many agricultural products can be sold or can be eaten, which makes it more difficult to assess their cash value. Additionally, agriculture is—per definition—the major source of income for smallholder farmers. Calculating their repayment capacity without taking the agricultural revenues into account is, therefore, impossible.

The *business experiences of a borrower* are often used as an indirect indicator for market conditions. Being in business for a certain amount of time shows the MFI that a potential client knows the market conditions and risks and knows where to buy inputs and sell his/her produce. An MFI, therefore, does not have to know all the potential risks of a specific market segment. (Churchill/Coster 2001, 36ff.; Klein et al. 1999, 19) Measuring the experience of a smallholder farmer solely through "time in business" is, however, not a sufficient indicator, as some smallholders might be subsistence farmers for a long time, but still not have the capacity and experience to commercially grow products and take on a loan. Loan officers thus need some knowledge of the different agricultural value chains and of both input and output markets to assess whether a smallholder has adequate experience and commercially grows his/her crops.

Table 5 shows that MFIs use different mechanisms during loan monitoring to *enforce loan repayments.* The mechanisms of group lending as well as frequent repayment installments, including their difficulties for smallholder farmers, were already explained in previous sections. The other listed mechanisms, for example, dynamic incentives and public repayments are also applicable to smallholder lending and are, therefore, not further elaborated.[38]

4.3 Reducing transaction costs in traditional microfinance

While the cost of money an MFI lends as well as the cost of loan default is proportional to the amount lent (and therefore small for microloans), transaction costs are

---

[38] Further explanations of these mechanisms can be found in Armendáriz/Morduch (2010, 140ff.).

not. Irrespective of the loan amount, the staff time for meeting the borrower for loan appraisal, processing the loan disbursement, and loan monitoring remains more or less the same. Consequently, high transaction costs are associated with lending small amounts to low-income clients. MFIs tackle this issue by charging higher, cost covering interest rates, but also by trying to reduce their operational costs through high volumes per loan officer as well as with highly standardized lending procedures that allow cutting down on loan assessment and monitoring costs. Group lending allows meeting many borrowers at the same time and thus helps loan officers to achieve high volumes. (Meyer 2011, 14ff.; Klein et al. 1999, 24ff.) As an in-depth analysis during loan assessment is costly for a lender as explained above, especially in relation to the low size of first-time micro-loans, client retention rates with increasing loan sizes are important to make microfinance profitable (Dorward et al. 2009, 11). During loan monitoring, MFIs often use regular repayments as an indicator for the well-being of a business, so that they do not have to check on the business in person unless a payment is overdue.

In agricultural lending for smallholder farmers, transaction costs are further increased through long distances in sparsely populated areas as well as through poor infrastructures. The additional information needed by loan officers as explained in the previous section further increases transaction costs. Additionally, frequent repayments cannot be used as indicator for the well-being of the agricultural business as the repayment installments are either met through another source of income or repayments are only made in one lump payment after harvest. Loan officers, therefore, have to regularly visit the farmers for loan monitoring. Even meeting smallholders in groups can probably not offset these higher costs. As explained in Section 7.1.2, covering these higher costs through higher interest rates can again pose other challenges.

5 Interim conclusion

There have been two main approaches to increase smallholders' productivity through access to credit in the past. After the highly subsidized agricultural lending programmes prevalent in the 1960s and 1970s mostly failed and many state agricultural development banks as well as credit programmes stopped operating, a new approach emerged and gave rise to a development often referred to as the "microfinance revolution" (Armendáriz/Morduch 2010, 8ff.). The new focus was on financially viable institutions offering a range of financial products to their clients. MFIs successfully developed innovative loan products and lending procedures that were able to mitigate the risks of lending money to low-income clients without traditional collateral. These new loan features as well as lending procedures (small loan amounts, short loan terms, high interest rates, joint group liability, staggered disbursements, etc.) make microcredit, however, most attractive for activities that need short-term working capital, have high turnovers and generate high profits on a regular basis. When taken for agricultural activities without adaption, borrowers often default as the microfinance requirements do not match their agricultural investments and cash flows.

Table 6 summarizes some of the common microfinance requirements and compares them to different investment options. The fields in Table 6 are coloured to indicate conformity between microfinance requirement and investment. It can be seen that the innovative approaches to reach low-income clients at manageable risks, while still being financially viable, lead to requirements that do not conform to most agricultural investments.

60   Traditional microfinance risk and cost management approaches

Table 6:   Traditional microfinance requirements and agricultural investments

Typical MFI requirements	Explanation	Petty trade	Milking cow	Crop loan	Agric. equipment
Investment amount	Small	*Small loan amount*	Small	Medium	Small/ Medium	Large
Delay between investment and return	Short	*Quick repayments*	Short	Medium to Short	Long	Very long
Percent return on investment	High	*Cost covering interest rates*	High	Medium	Medium to low	Low
Lump size of return (low to high)	Low	*Frequent repayments*	Low	Low	High	High
Centrality of investment to household (hh) income	Low	*Diversified hh income*	Low	Medium	Medium to high	Medium to high
Time sensitivity of investment	Low	*Staggered loan disbursement within group*	Low	Low	High	High
Distance between clients	Short	*High volumes per loan officers*	Short	depends	Long (mostly)	Long (mostly)
Infrastructure	Good	*High volumes per loan officers*	Good	depends	Bad (mostly)	Bad (mostly)

Note: the first column contains both the requirement name and its value; the Explanation column appears in italics. The table has been transcribed with seven columns: Typical MFI requirements | value | Explanation | Petty trade | Milking cow | Crop loan | Agric. equipment.

Source: own table based on Harper 2005.

In addition to traditional microfinance challenges, MFIs that wish to offer agricultural finance for smallholder farmers face further risks and costs, such as high costs for reaching farmers in remote rural areas with poor infrastructures and high external risks (weather, plant pests, and diseases) that cannot yet be mitigated through insurance products. Market prices for agricultural products are also highly volatile and put the smallholder as well as the MFI at an additional risk. Furthermore, external risks pose a high co-variant risk as they affect all smallholders in a given area. Due to these reasons, many MFIs are highly reluctant to serve smallholder farmers and rural areas and agriculture are still highly underserved in SSA.

There are, however, a number of MFIs in SSA that managed to cope with these challenges and successfully offer financial services to smallholder farmers. The following chapters will look at their different approaches and analyse how they changed their loan features and adapted their lending procedures in a way that mitigates the credit risk of lending to uncollateralized clients *and* suits agricultural investments.

6 Overview of interviewed MFIs and their agricultural lending strategies

Agricultural finance for smallholder farmers is provided by a range of MFIs with different institutional backgrounds in SSA. The empirical research is mainly based on the analysis of the agricultural lending experience of eight MFIs in four different countries, that is, Uganda, Kenya, Benin, and Cameroon.[39]

6.1 Indicators and agricultural loan products of interviewed MFIs

All interviewed MFIs have several years of experience in offering agricultural loans to smallholder farmers. They differ, however, in their institutional background, size, regional outreach, as well as in their number of clients as can be seen in Table 7.

Table 7 splits the interviewed MFIs[40] into the already explained three categories: (1) commercial banks (CBs) offering microfinance and agricultural finance for smallholder farmers as part of their overall portfolio. (2) Microfinance companies (MFCs) purely concentrating on micro-clients and the provision of microfinance services. The interviewed MFCs are spin-offs of NGOs and are now trying to reach financial sustainability as standalone institutions. (3) Membership-based financial institutions (MBFIs) offering a range of financial products solely to their members.

---

[39] In the present and the following chapters, references to interview partners will be made in footnotes to ensure optimum readability. Interview partner will be quoted with their institution and position/ job title; for privacy reasons names are not disclosed.

[40] Independent of their institutional type, all interviewed institutions offer microfinance products and are thus generally referred to as MFIs in this paper.

62 Overview of interviewed MFIs and their agricultural lending strategies

Table 7: Comparison of indicators of interviewed MFIs in 2011*

	MFI/Country		Established[1]	Total assets (MM USD)[2]	Gross loan portfolio (MM USD)[2]	Deposits (MM USD)[2]	Clients (thousands)	Branches
CB	Equity Bank	KE	1984/1993	2,116	1,301	1,501	7,151	186
	CRDB	UG	1983/1993	386	215	284	1,134	39
MFC	Faulu	KE	1991	62	40	7	226	96
	RUCREF	UG	1993/2000	n/a	1	0	6	7
	Juhudi Kilimo	KE	2004/2009	3	2	0	7	8
MBFI	Agaru SACCO	UG	2002	2	1	1	9	4
	FECECAM[3]	BJ	1976	100	56	85	641	108
	MC²s[3]	CM	1992	83	28	62	132	90

[1] Two dates imply that the MFI initially started their operation under a different institutional set-up. The second date represents the start of operation under its recent institutional set-up (i.e. Equity Bank started as a building society, CERUB as a credit trust; RUCREF and Juhudi Kilimo as NGO credit programmes).
[2] Financial statements were in local currency. Exchange rates from 31 December 2011 (31 December 2010) were used for conversion.
[3] Figures are for the whole federation of member-based institutions and not for single institutions, date of establishment represents opening of first MBFI.
*The 2011 financial statements were not available for RUCREF; 2010 data were used.
Sources: own table based on financial reports of MFIs, MFI websites and interviews with MFIs

Table 8 does not include indicators of portfolio quality and/or the financial viability of the interviewed MFIs, as suitable comparable numbers or indicators were not available. The basis of calculation of NPLs or PAR, for example, differs, at times significantly, among the interviewed MFIs making it difficult to compare. All institutions have, however, been operating for some time (see date of establishment) which implies to some extent their degree of (financial) stability.

The different sizes, varying institutional backgrounds, and different approaches to agricultural lending also have their effect on the agricultural portfolios and loan products of interviewed MFIs, as can be seen in Table 8. Table 8 separates loans according to their loan term. Rows without separation between short- and medium-term loans indicate that the respective MFI offers loans that would fall under medium-term loans based on their maximum loan term, but are often taken as a short-term loan, for example, for farm inputs. A complete overview of the loans and their respective loan features can be found in Chapter 7. Chapter 7 will further elaborate on the respective loan features of the interviewed MFIs and how they adapted these features to agricultural lending to smallholder farmers.

Table 8: Overview of agricultural loan portfolio and loan products of interviewed MFIs*

	MFI	Agricultural loan portfolio (MM USD)[1] / (as percentage of total loan portfolio)	Short-term loans (≤12 months)	Medium-term loans (≥12 months)
CB	Equity Bank	39.5 (3%)	(1) Farm input: loan for general farming needs (inputs, farm machinery, social needs) (2) Farm inputs and equipment for small cereal and horticulture farmers (3) Micro-enterprises dealing in all agric. related production and agri-business activities (farming, livestock, pastoralists, fishing) (4) Warehouse receipts	(5) Commercial agriculture: input and equipment for larger farmers, pastoralists, and fishermen (6) Farm inputs and equipment for larger cereal farmers (7) Agribusiness loan for cereal value chain (agro-dealers, input manufacturers, etc.) (8) Farm development (buildings, fences, etc.) (9) Purchase of modern agricultural equipment
CB	CRDB	26.5 (12%)	(1) General loan for agricultural production, processing, marketing, animal husbandry, bee keeping, and fishery	(2) Animal traction (3) Microleasing
MFC	Faulu	0.6 (2%)	(1) Agricultural production loan for cereal farmers (2) Livestock loan for dairy farmers (3) Warehouse receipts for cereal farmers (in planning)	No medium-term loans
MFC	RUCREF	n/a		Under review in 2011
MFI	Juhudi Kilimo	2.1 (100%)	(1) Loan for assets along the dairy value chain (2) General asset loan for livestock (rabbits, poultry, pigs), agricultural equipment, and farm transport	
MBFI	Agaru SACCO	0.4 (42%)	(1) General agricultural production loan (2) Animal traction (3) Tractor loan (4) Drip irrigation (pilot) (5) Warehouse receipts (pilot) (≤6 months)	
MBFI	CLCAM (Pehunco, Kouandé)	n/a (24%)[2]	(1) General loan for agricultural production, equipment, and animal husbandry (2) COMPACI loan for cotton farmers' production, equipment, and animal traction	
MBFI	MC²s	4.5 (16%)	(1) General loan for agricultural production, equipment, and livestock	

[1] It is important to note that the level of agricultural loan portfolio is not constant over the year, but highly corresponds to the agricultural seasons. The portfolio depicted below represents the situation as of 31 December and is, therefore, not totally representative for the overall amount of agricultural lending of the respective MFIs.
[2] Of the new loan issued in 2011, 24% were agricultural loans.

* This overview was compiled on the basis of information coming from interviews conducted from June to September 2011. Some MFIs may have since changed their agricultural loan portfolio.

Source: own table based on interviews with MFIs, MFI websites; MFIs' financial (annual) reports.

64 Overview of interviewed MFIs and their agricultural lending strategies

As will be shown in the following sections, the institutional set up confronts MFIs with further challenges and opportunities, in addition to the challenges already depicted in Chapter 3. While CBs have sound financial knowledge and well-established management and information systems, their branches are often located in urban areas or rural centres. Reaching out to smallholder farmers is, therefore, more expensive for them. Understanding the agricultural sector, the mentality of smallholder farmers, and gaining the trust of these farmers can be an additional challenge for CBs. MFCs are closer to smallholders, as they belong to their target group of the low-income population. Their commercial drive for profitability, their need to borrow money on the financial market, as most of them are credit-only institutions, as well as their often limited branch network might drive them away from agricultural lending as a concentration on urban micro-entrepreneurs is perceived to be more profitable and less risky. MBFIs, on the other hand, are deeply rooted in their rural communities, where they can draw on local knowledge, social ties, and volunteer staff. While this greatly reduces their operational costs, elected loan committees with little economic background and a limited staff size can destabilize the entire institution.

Aside from these varying institutional backgrounds, it is interesting to see that the different MFIs had some common or similar learning experiences as they developed agricultural lending for smallholder farmers. First, all of the MFIs realized that agricultural lending to smallholder farmer requires specific agricultural knowledge of management (to develop appropriate loans) as well as loan officers (to follow specific procedures during loan assessment and monitoring). Almost all interviewed MFIs received support from development partners or governmental programmes to achieve this. Secondly, CBs and MFCs started and/or still conduct their agricultural lending by focusing on specific value chains that they have analysed and thus thoroughly understand. Knowing the crop as well as its growing patterns, input needs and marketing channels helps to develop appropriate loan products and tailor the loan assessment and monitoring in a way that can mitigate many risks. Thirdly, CBs and MFCs only started to move into agricultural lending 4–15 years after the establishment of their respective institution.

The interviewed institutions, their approaches to agricultural lending as well as their respective challenges will be elaborated on in the following.

6.2 Commercial banks

Equity Bank (Kenya)[41] and Centenary Rural Development Bank of Uganda (CRDB) are registered CBs offering a wide range of financial products to clients of all income levels in their respective countries. While CBs in SSA traditionally do not offer microfinance products (Beck et al. 2011, 89), Equity Bank and CRDB have included the provision of microfinance services into their corporate philosophy since their establishment (Equity Bank 2013a, CRDB 2013a). Both institutions started their lending activities to smallholder farmers several years after their successful establishment as viable commercial institutions and in promising areas and/or within promising value chains. They only spread to other branches and additional loan products after gaining sufficient experiences.

CRDB chose its Mbale branch in 1998 for piloting smallholder lending, because it was located in an area where high-value crops were grown and the environment was supportive for such an endeavour (available and well-developed markets for agricultural produce, relatively constant price levels, good agricultural extension services, developed land ownership and good and relatively constant rainfall and production, high population density) (Ministry of Finance/CRDB 2002, 22ff.; Kyanika Nsibambi 2010, 41). Even though the conditions were favourable, CRDB faced high default rates in their first years of the pilot. These were caused by dropping prices, insufficient loan appraisal due to inexperienced loan officers, poor credit culture by clients, and a rough terrain that made recovery difficult. They successfully faced this challenge through tough recovery procedures to educated clients that loans are no government handouts and through the employment of more agricultural loan officers with a background in agriculture. Since then, CRDB has spread its agricultural lending activities "slowly but surely to other branches" (Kyanika Nsibambi 2010, 42). Table 8 shows that CRDB offers three different agricultural loan products: a general short-term loan for agriculture as well as two loans for asset finance (animal traction and microleasing[42]). In 2011, CRDB had an agri-

---

[41] Equity Bank Group also started to operate in other African Countries. This paper, however, solely focuses on the Kenyan operations.

[42] CRDB offers microleasing as long-term asset finance (loan term of up to 5 years) for microclients within but also outside the agricultural sector. Assets are leased to individuals or organizations that pay periodic rentals. Once all agreed rentals have been paid, the customer automatically owns the asset, while it is still the bank's property before this period ends. It is thus a fully collateralized product and since the leased product is insured, a customer can only loose what s/he is leasing and not any of his/her household items or property. (CRDB 2013b)

cultural loan portfolio of USD 26.5 million, which corresponds to 12% of the overall loan portfolio.

Equity Bank gained their first agricultural lending experiences through lending to small commercial tea and dairy farmers.[43] Both value chains are well structured and smallholder farmers earn steady incomes through regular milk sales and regular purchasing agreements with the tea buying company that enable them to regularly repay their loans. Additionally, both products are secured by agribusiness contracts (Pearce/Reinsch 2006, 44). According to the Agribusiness General Manager of Equity Bank, developing loan products and lending procedures for these value chains was thus a good and easy start.[44] In 2005, Equity's overall lending business was internally reorganized into sector-based lending and agricultural lending became a separate sector with its own internal structure and staff. In 2008, the first group comprising entirely of agriculturalists was hired to professionalize the agricultural lending business and today, more than 200 loan officers with agricultural background offer agricultural finance to smallholder farmers in all of Equity Bank's branches in Kenya. Equity Bank offers nine different short- and medium-term agricultural loan products, as can be seen in Table 8. They do not offer loans for specific agricultural value chains, but offer slightly different loan terms to different target groups (general farmers, cereal and horticulture farmers, and micro-enterprises)[45] and for different types of assets (equipment and farm development). They also offer warehouse receipts.[46] Looking at the description of their farm input loans, one can see that they not only cover agricultural activities but also social needs. Equity Bank is the only interviewed MFI that defines agricultural loans as "loans exposed to agriculture related risks"[47] rather than loans for agricultural purposes. Thus, all loans that are mainly repaid through agricultural activities (e.g. a school or emergency loan taken by a smallholder farmer) fall under agriculture and,

---

[43] The author does not know when exactly lending to tea and dairy farmers started. It can only be assumed that it must have started some time before 2000, because a 2001 market survey came to the conclusion that Equity only targeted tea and dairy farmers at this time (Coetzee et al. 2002, 15).
[44] Agribusiness General Manager, Equity Bank.
[45] Within this group they also differentiate between small and larger farmers. While small farmers only receive short-term credit, larger farmers have access to medium-term loans.
[46] Warehouses securely store agricultural products until they can be sold at higher prices. Farmers can receive receipts stating the quantity and quality of the stored product and use this receipt as collateral for a loan (see Section 7.1).
[47] Agribusiness General Manager, Equity Bank.

therefore, also have the agricultural loan features (interest rate, repayment schedule, etc.). This enables smallholders to access social needs loans when they would otherwise have difficulties in accessing these loans due to the restrictive loan features (e.g. quick repayment shortly after disbursal). Furthermore, it also reduces the risk for Equity Bank, since it avoids loan diversion:

> "We make them understand that we finance all the purposes. (...) If I only give loans to finance farm inputs and as I oriented myself to only that facility of farm input, it means (...) they [smallholders, the author] may divert the funds they were supposed to use for farming input. But to mitigate that it would mean that you're able to meet all their needs. (...) Provided they are in the position to serve your facilities."[48]

Thus, also these social needs loans fall within the agricultural portfolio of Equity Bank, which was at USD 39.5 million in 2011. This corresponds to 3% of their overall loan portfolio.[49]

Equity Bank offers a greater number of loan products available under a variety of conditions than is the case with CRDB, which only offers three different loan products for smallholders. There are, however, some important similarities between the two. First, both offer loan products within their short-term loans that cover working capital (e.g. inputs) as well as assets [e.g. farm machinery (Equity), animal husbandry (CRDB)]. Secondly, in addition to offering loan products for farmers, that is, the agricultural production stage, they also provide loans for other activities along agricultural value chains, for example, input provision, processing, and marketing. They do so to ensure that financial constraints do not hinder the chain from functioning well (Kyanika Nsibambi 2010, 44) as "a [value] chain is as strong as its weakest link".[50] Thirdly, their agricultural loan product terms are not tailored to specific value chains or crops. This can be explained by the fact that their loan product development takes place in the head office and that both banks offer their agricultural loan products at almost every branch, hence in different agro-ecological zones with many different crops and value chains. They therefore developed several rather general loan products and then tailor the loans to the client's

---

[48] Relationship Officer for Agriculture, Equity Bank, Kikuyu branch.
[49] The small share that agriculture represents in the overall portfolio is due to the enormous growth rates of Equity Bank over the last years: During 2005–2010 their agricultural portfolio increased yearly by around 66%, but their share of agriculture portfolio remained at around 3–4% during the same period due to their large overall increase of gross loan portfolio (calculated on basis of Equity Bank's Financial Statements 2005–2010).
[50] Agribusiness General Manager, Equity Bank.

need and the agricultural situation at each branch. They conduct a thorough market survey at every new branch, in which they assess the agricultural situation (existing crops and their commercial potential, crop cycles, existence of agricultural markets and extension services, cultural and land issues, etc.). Based on this assessment, which is often done in collaboration with external partners, such as the Ministry of Agriculture (MoA) or development partners, it is decided which kind of farmers and crops can be financed in a given area and the loan assessment and monitoring criteria are adapted accordingly.[51]

6.3 Microfinance companies

All three interviewed microfinance companies are commercially driven companies with a social mission to empower the economically active (rural) poor by providing financial services in an economically sustainable way.[52] Started as NGO spin-offs, they are now independent commercial institutions offering credits-only to low-income clients (only Faulu acquired a deposit-taking licence in 2009 and has been offering savings accounts since then). Their business strategies are, however, quite different. Faulu and RUCREF have a limited portfolio in agriculture. They mainly offer short-term working capital loans and experienced similar challenges when they started their agricultural lending business. Juhudi Kilimo, on the other hand, has its entire credit portfolio in asset-based finance for smallholder agriculture. All three focus on specific value chains, in which they have in-depth knowledge instead of offering loan products to farmers from many different value chains.

RUCREF was founded in 1993 as a microfinance programme of VEDCO, an NGO supporting subsistence farmers and micro-entrepreneurs in the Luwero Triangle area.[53] In 2000, the programme became a separate entity and registered as an MFI. Even though RUCREF was aimed at smallholder farmers *and* micro-entrepreneurs, they quickly concentrated on retail, commercial, and business lending as they were striving for financial sustainability. According to the Agricultural Product Specialist of RUCREF, it was easier to establish a viable business by lending to small commerce and business clients, because their turnovers are higher, risks are limited, and the mechanism (loan features, lending procedures) are well

---

[51] Agribusiness General Manager, Equity Bank; Seibel 2003, 43.
[52] Agricultural Product Specialist, RUCREF; Juhudi Kilimo 2013a; Faulu 2013a.
[53] Luwero Triangle is an area north of Kampala in Uganda that was devastated by a civil war between the National Resistance Army and the government between 1981 and 1986.

known. Hence, RUCREF offered typical micro-credits with features as described in Chapter 4. They also offered these loans to smallholder farmers, but without much success:

> "It was just a copy and paste. From business bringing the same ideas to agriculture. (...) When they [the smallholders] would come to us, we would give them credit but in conditions that were not favourable to them. Because RUCREF wanted to be profitable. All our aim was to make this institution a sustainable institution. So (...) we ended up giving them the credit in agricultural financing, but in a way that was not pleasant to them and which was not helping them solve their problems."[54]

Offering loans with traditional microfinance loan features to smallholders had different consequences. Many smallholders were not eligible for RUCREF's loans even though RUCREF was initially founded with the purpose of also addressing their credit needs. Other smallholders who did receive credits with traditional microfinance loan features were often not able to repay these. PAR among agricultural loans was thus high and RUCREF's staff perceived smallholder lending as very risky compared to general microfinance loans. Due to these experiences, RUCREF's board and management decided in late 2010 to establish an agricultural lending department to review their approach with the goal of meeting the needs of smallholder farmers in Luwera region while at the same time being mindful about its own financial sustainability.[55]

Faulu had similar experience when they started agricultural lending. Initially starting as a loan scheme in 1991 that targeted the economically active poor in slums of Nairobi, they encountered a demand for loans by smallholder farmers through their branch expansion into rural areas. In 2002, they therefore started agricultural lending to smallholder farmers. Due to the agronomic situation around their braches, most of their agricultural loans were input loans for cereals (maize, wheat, and rice), as well as some loans for dairy farmers. Their loan portfolio was, however, not solely restricted to these value chains. Unlike RUCREF, Faulu did not just offer their traditional micro-credits to these farmers, but adapted some loan features, for example, adding a grace period and offering loan repayment in one lump sum after harvest for cereal farmers. Their overall lending approach remained, however, the same: "We did not prepare our staff to take care of that kind of lend-

---

[54] Agricultural Product Specialist, RUCREF.
[55] Agricultural Product Specialist, RUCREF.

ing because we thought we can do it just as every other business."[56] The initial loan uptake was good and 3 years later, Faulu had 55,000 clients in agriculture, including 30,000 within cereal production. External events such as post-election violence with burned fields, a heavy drought, and also loan diversion and general loan default not caused by external circumstances led to a high number of NPLs within their agricultural lending business and especially among their cereal loans. They therefore suspended their agricultural lending activities 3 years after they started to rethink their approach.

During their review process, both institutions realized that agricultural lending to smallholder farmers requires more than just changing some loan features (such as repayment schedule). They both followed a similar approach: the creation of a specific department for agricultural lending within their MFI, the conduction of thorough market research, the adaption of their lending procedures for agriculture, a pilot of agricultural products for smallholders and agricultural training for their staff.

Within Faulu, the position of an Agribusiness Development Manager was created to do profound market research on agribusiness and the cereal value chain, in particular. The research included many field visits and conversations with cereal farmers to understand their businesses, challenges, and their financial needs. Furthermore, Faulu assessed the challenges and financial needs of the entire cereal value chain. Following this, a pilot with around 5,000 cereal farmers that included a more holistic lending approach was launched. The loan assessment and loan monitoring procedures were changed (e.g. assessing the whole household income and monthly repayment of interest; for more see Chapter 7) and loan officers received agricultural training. Additionally, Faulu introduced compulsory weather insurance and started to cooperate with other value chain actors (agro-dealers; national warehouses) to address general problems in the cereal value chain (e.g. low prices after harvest; bad quality of inputs) as well as loan diversion (e.g. by paying directly to the agro-dealer). Their pilot for cereal loans was still ongoing in 2011, but the Agribusiness Development Manager was confident that the new approach would result in lower PAR. Faulu also continued to offer some loans to dairy farmers, as can be seen in Table 8. Since the dairy value chain around Faulu branches is well developed, this kind of lending is less risky, easier to monitor and more similar to tradi-

---

[56] Agribusiness Development Manager, Faulu.

tional microfinance, since dairy farmers have a regular income from daily milk sales.

RUCREF's newly founded agricultural lending department reviewed their agricultural portfolio and lending procedures and realized the need for a proper market analysis of all value chains they are involved in. Their survey included farmer interviews and discussions with extension services and the agricultural ministry. The results made them realize that agriculture has specifics they had not taken into account so far:

> "(…) in commercial trade once you give someone money, you don't have to follow up with seasons, you don't have to follow up with markets, it's more or less the business plan which tells you whether the business is profitable or not. But in agricultural lending, and this is why so many people are not in it, there are additionalities."[57]

These additionalities include seasons, the existence of supporting services (e.g. extension services), access to input and output markets and the general organization and structure of the value chain as well as the professionalism of other value chain actors. Knowing all stakeholders interacting with the farmers (e.g. extension services, input provider, buyer, NGOs supporting farmers) and cooperating with them is, therefore, crucial for agricultural lending, according to the Agricultural Product Specialist of RUCREF. The research was still ongoing in 2011, which is why RUCREF's agricultural loan products are not included in Table 8 and in the following chapters.

Juhudi Kilimo's background and business strategy towards agricultural lending is different from that of Faulu and RUCREF. Founded as an initiative within the K-Rep Development Agency (KDA)[58] in 2004 and operating as an independent for-profit company since 2009, its focus has always been on financing agricultural assets that offer an immediate extra source of income for farmers (Juhudi Kilimo 2013b). Farmers are thus able to repay their loans through the new asset, while retaining the asset afterwards adds incrementally to their balance sheets. Assets are collateralized, meaning farmers can only loose what the MFI added, which reduces the farmer's risk of over indebtedness and greater poverty. Additionally, the

---

[57] Agricultural Product Specialist, RUCREF.
[58] KDA is the research and development arm of the K-Rep group. It specializes in microfinance (product) development. Registered as an NGO in 1987, KDA initially supported other NGOs through grants and technical assistance before broadening its activities in 1989 to include the direct delivery of loans, research, and training. (KDA 2013)

asset is insured to protect the farmer from any harsh business losses due to, for example, the death of a cow.[59]

It took Juhudi Kilimo 3–4 years to develop its specific product range. During this phase, Juhudi Kilimo was still a non-profit business belonging to KDA and receiving financial and technical support of several development partners. Loan products for different assets were tested (e.g. fishing nets, dairy cows, etc.) before KDA/Juhudi Kilimo decided to focus on the dairy value chain and, in areas of the chain that were well developed (existing cooling plants, milk transport, etc.).[60] Once the business model was proven and began to take off, KDA decided to spin it off as an independent entity and Juhudi Kilimo Limited was founded. Today the MFC Juhudi Kilimo perceives itself as a social business: a sustainable and profitable business offering services that also improve the livelihoods of smallholders. At the times of the interview, Juhudi Kilimo had 70% of their portfolio within the dairy value chain, but also offered a loan product for other value chain products, as can be seen in Table 8. The main challenge it faced was to manage its growth and establish adequate information and management systems to allow control of the performance of loan officers, for example, and to establish performance-based incentives.[61]

6.4 Membership-based financial institutions

The interviewed membership-based financial institutions follow yet another philosophy. Their primary objective is not aimed at profitability, but at empowering the rural population and integrating them into the development process through the provision of financial services. MBFIs are micro-banks, created, owned, and managed by the members of the community. They have a limited number of salaried staff members and banking tasks are taken over by elected members. Due to their low-level institutional system and their ability to access local information on potential borrowers, their (transaction) costs are comparatively low, which is why they can operate in less-favoured areas unreached by formal banks or micro-finance companies. (World Bank 2006, 33) This allows them to be present in very remote rural areas, where no other providers of financial services exist.

---

[59] Consultant for performance management, Juhudi Kilimo; Juhudi Kilimo 2013b.
[60] Consultant for performance management, Juhudi Kilimo.
[61] Consultant for performance management, Juhudi Kilimo.

Agaru Savings and Credit Co-operative (SACCO) started its operation in 2002 in Kalongo, Pader district, in the north of Uganda with the support of the World Council of Credit Unions (WOCCU).[62] At the time, Pader district was still heavily hit by the ongoing insurgent activities of the Lord's Resistance Army (LRA) and people were living in camps around Kalongo town. Agaru SACCO's aim was to provide a safe place for people's savings in a war-affected area, where no other financial institutions existed and to "give back to the community traumatized by the LRA insurgency for long years, through the provision of access to financial services and thus empower them to become economically active" (Wehnert/Heine 2010, 14). Agaru SACCO emphasizes savings culture over the provision of loans (Agaru SACCO 2010, 1).

Having started off with one office and four employees in a refugee camp, Agaru SACCO today has four branches, approximately 24 salaried staff members, 9,000 members, and USD 1.2 million in savings. Membership is acquired by buying at least one share and is open to groups, individuals, and institutions of Uganda. Members receive interest on savings as well as a shareholder dividend and have access to different loan products. Board members and loan committee members are elected and come from within the community. (Wehnert/Heine 2010, 15ff.)

From the very beginning, Agaru SACCO offered its general loan for agricultural production: a general loan for different kinds of agricultural production needs of smallholder farmer growing different crops with a loan term of 18 months (Table 8). As most of their members were and still are smallholder farmers engaged in agriculture "as their only source of economic survival" (Wehnert/Heine 2010, 13), offering agricultural loans for smallholders was not a business decision to be considered, but a necessity. The agricultural activities of members were, however, limited as they lived in camps at the time. This made loan monitoring easier, as their fields were closely located around the camp. When people started to move back to their land around 2007, agricultural loan demand highly increased and Agaru SACCO was faced with various challenges: poor infrastructure led to inadequate access to input and output markets, missing storage facilities increased post-harvest loss and farmers often had no other choice than selling their crops at low prices to middlemen. Agricultural extension services were inexistent, smallholders lacked financial education, and basic farm bookkeeping all made loan appraisal time con-

---

[62] Agaru SACCO was registered as a co-operative in 2001 under the 1991 Co-operative Statute, but only began its operation in 2002 (Wormgoor/Ssenyimba 2007, 1).

suming and costly; the dependency syndrome of people who lived in camps for years was high and many thought they received their loans as handouts. Furthermore, tracking borrowers was often difficult as many did not resettle at their farmlands immediately but kept moving around.[63] Additionally, Agaru SACCO lacked experienced personnel in agricultural loan development, piloting, and monitoring:

> "Another challenge was that within ourselves we didn't have enough knowledge of how much money can be required to plant maybe one acre of let's say rice. From the beginning up to the level of harvesting it. Until that challenge was addressed by recruiting people that were specialized in agriculture."[64]

A major drought that led to high crop losses in 2009 exacerbated the situation and led to overdue payments on 48% of outstanding loans in December 2009 (Opio Ogal 2009, 133).

In recent years, Agaru SACCO worked to address these and other challenges with the help of development partners. The Italian Cooperation funded, for example, the employment of 10 agricultural extension officers for 1 year in 2009. They were tasked with training smallholders and developing new agricultural loan products, adapting loan features and providing agricultural training to loan officers to enhance their skills in proper loan assessment and monitoring for agriculture as well as advising farmers on good agricultural practices.[65] Some of these extension workers were later hired as loan officers by Agaru SACCO. New loan products were also piloted, such as animal traction and tractor loan, drip irrigation and a warehouse receipt system to address poor storage and low prices after harvest (Table 8). (Opio Ogal 2009, 133; Agaru SACCO 2010, 6ff.)

While Agaru SACCO has no umbrella organization offering support services, the **Caisses Locales de Crédit Agricole Mutual (CLCAM)** are part of the largest credit union network covering the whole of Benin. Their umbrella organization is called Faîtière des Caisses d'Epargne et de Crédit Agricole Mutuel (FECECAM) and aims at providing financial services to rural farmers.

---

[63] Manager Loans and Agricultural System Administrator, Agaru SACCO; Opio Ogal 2009, 134ff.
[64] Loan Officer for Agriculture, Agaru SACCO, Kalongo branch.
[65] Agaru SACCO is also supported by a range of other organizations such as the German Society for International Cooperation (GIZ), the Department for International Development (DFID), WOCCU, ZOA International (Agaru SACCO 2010, 14ff.).

FECECAM was created in 1993, but the roots of the CLCAMs can be traced back to 1976, when they were attached to the state bank Caisse Nationale de Crédit Agricole (CNCA).[66] After the collapse of CNCA in 1987, the credit unions network was rehabilitated and reorganized in 1989 with enormous donor support. Regional CLCAMs called URCLCAMs were established to support local CLCAMs. In 1993, FECECAM started its operation and has since been the national representative of the network. It also offers supporting services to URLCAMs and CLCAMs (e.g. training of elected board members and supervisors; development of new loan products) and monitors the performance of the credit unions. (Westercam 1999, 5ff.) Due to the disastrous experience with the state bank CNCA, CLCAMs have made savings mobilization, autonomy, and freedom from external lines of credit "into articles of faith" (Morris 1995, 7).

Today 108 CLCAMs exist in the whole of Benin with a total of 641,000 members. CLCAMs are owned and managed by their members through an elected board of directors and a board of supervisors. They are supported by a limited number of one to six salaried staff. Elected representatives often come from the upper social classes, that is, educated farmers with better farming equipment than the average farmer, retired civil servants, etc. (Westercam 1999, 9ff.). In 2003, the World Bank conducted a performance assessment of CLCAMs and reported the following challenges: many elected board members were unfamiliar with the workings of a financial institution and the training provided to new board members was not sufficient to provide them with adequate skills. The fact that board members were able to obtain loans which they did not intend to repay was an additional challenge at some CLCAMs. Long delays for obtaining credits and loan terms that are not adapted to producers' needs were also mentioned. (World Bank 2003, 4ff.)

---

[66] This set-up is an example of the old paradigm of agricultural finance. According to Morris (1995, 6ff.) the attachment of CLCAMs to CNCA "was in principle intended to provide the CNCA-Bénin with a network of rural institutions through which it could channel donor subsidies and lines of credit intended to finance crop loans and promote rural economic development. At the same time, these institutions would serve as repositories of farmers' earnings from agricultural projects and would permit the system's 'excess liquidity' to be 'managed.' In fact, the CNCA-Bénin's tutelage of the (...) CLCAM system accomplished just the opposite. The external funding was woefully and corruptly mismanaged, and more often than not the rural populations that were its intended beneficiaries never had access to it. Rather than mobilizing and safeguarding members' savings, members' savings into the CNCA-Bénin system were lost when the bank was closed."

76 Overview of interviewed MFIs and their agricultural lending strategies

To improve the access of cotton farmers to short- and medium-term credit, COMPACI began cooperating with CLCAMs in northern Benin in 2009. COMPACI cotton farmers perceived the interest rates of CLCAM's general agricultural loan (Table 8) as being too high. Additionally, there was a lack of medium-term loans for agricultural equipment, as some CLCAMs lacked funds or shied away from the higher risk of medium-term loans, even though their general loan could be extended for up to 24 months (and at some CLCAMs even 36 months). A complex set-up incorporating several value chain actors aims at resolving these challenges and is described in Section 8.2. In addition to the COMPACI loan, CLCAMs also offer a general agricultural production loan (similar to the COMPACI loan but at higher interest rates).

In Cameroon, a similar system of credit unions exists, namely a network of 90 **MC²s** today. While the internal structure of MC²s is comparable to CLCAMs (membership-based credit unions with elected boards and loan committees and a limited number of salaried staff), the overall set-up is different. The MC² network was initiated by Dr Paul K. Fokam, with the aim of integrating the rural sector into the development process by using local resources and by respecting local cultures and values. MC² therefore stands for achieving victory over poverty by pooling the means (M) and competences (C) of the community (C), hence $M \times C \times C = MC^2$. The model that began with this idea has been developed in various communities since 1992 (date of the creation of the first MC²) with the technical support of the NGO ADAF and Afriland First Bank (a commercial Cameroonian bank). (ADAF 2013a) While the single MC²s are independent, member-owned and -managed financial institutions, they are supported and controlled by ADAF as well as Afriland First Bank. ADAF's role is to support the establishment of new MC²s as well as train, support, and control the existing MC²s and connect MC²s to international development partners.[67] Afriland First Bank conducts external audits, trains employees in banking services, secures MC²'s savings, and offers refinancing possibilities

---

[67] The new establishment of an MC² follows three steps: (1) Conduction of a feasibility study and awareness raising among the people of a community and local elites; (2) establishment of a social fund (around 15 million FCFA, USD 30,000, have to be collected before an MC² opens); (3) setting up the general assembly, election of bodies, recruitment of staff; opening of branch, mobilizing of savings, and deposits. An MC² generally reaches a stable situation after 4–5 years. (Mees/Bombda 2006, 3ff.).

as well as additional banking services (e.g. international money transfer) that MC² members can access through their MC²s.[68]

MC²s face similar challenges as the other MBFIs: while the lean staff structure reduces costs, committee members are not always qualified to do proper loan appraisals, even though manuals on key indicators and procedures for loan appraisal and monitoring exist. It also happens that loans are granted to respected persons of the community and/or family members without proper analysis or that loan repayment for these people is rarely enforced.[69] ADAF staff, therefore, attends some loan committee meetings and develop recommendations for the election of loan committee members (e.g. one elected member needs to have a financial, another an agronomic background, etc.).

Even though most MC²s are located in remote rural areas where agriculture is a main economic activity, many MC²s were reluctant to lend to smallholder farmers due to high perceived risks as well as a lack of knowledge on how to reduce agriculture-related risks through specific loan features and lending procedures. A government-funded programme (PAD-MC²) started in 2004 to address some of these challenges. The programme provided resources for on-lending to smallholder farmers at low interest rates (coupled with the requirement to achieve repayment rates above 90%) as well as technical assistance, for example, studies on simple indicators for different agricultural products (such as number of fertilizer bags for one acre of different agricultural products, length of different growing cycles, etc.), agronomic training of loan officers, and material support, for example, motorcycles to be able to make farm visits.

---

[68] More information on the link between the MC² network, ADAF, and Afriland First Bank can be found in Mees/Bomda 2006.
[69] Executive Secretary, ADAF.

7 Risk mitigation through adapted loan products and lending procedures

While the previous Chapter 6 outlined the different strategic motivations behind the MFIs' approaches to agricultural lending, all interviewed MFIs shared similar experiences in the process of adapting loan features and lending procedures to agricultural finance for smallholder farmers, which will be presented in this chapter. As loan interest rates (*i*) are an important part of loan design, directly linked to covering loan costs and on top of that subject of controversial political discussion, they will be examined in greater detail in Section 7.1.2.

7.1 Loan features of agricultural production loans

Tables 9 and 10 provide an overview of the interviewed MFIs' agricultural loan products and their specific features, such as loan amount, loan term, repayment schedule, collateral requirements, and interest rates. Loans are separated by their loan terms, thus into short-term loans with a loan term of up to 12 months and medium-/long-term loans with loan periods longer than 12 months. The separation in short- and medium-/long-term loans was not completely straightforward for all MFIs, so the following exceptions were made: short-term loans also include Agaru SACCO's general agricultural loan, even though it has a loan term of 18 months, as it was mostly used for shorter-term working capital.[70] CLCAM's general agricultural loan as well as their COMPACI loan (loan term of a maximum of 24 months) were used to finance both short-term working capital and medium-/long-term agricultural assets. The same loan could, therefore, be quoted as a short-term or as medium-/long-term loan. For reasons of space, it was only listed once under medium-/long-term loans. Additionally, Agaru SACCO's drip irrigation loan as well as Equity Bank's loan for farm inputs and equipment for larger cereal farmers and its agribusiness loan for cereal value chains (agro-dealers, input manufacturers, etc.) are not included in the tables, as they either do not target smallholder farmers (Equity Bank) or were just pilots and not yet finally designed (Agaru SACCO).

It is also important to note that even though the question on loan features was present in all interviews, some specific information, for example, on further features, might not have been mentioned during interviews and the table might, therefore, lack some information. Additionally, the information stems from June to September 2011 and loan products or their loan features may have since changed.

---
[70] Loan Officer for Agriculture, Agaru SACCO, Kalongo branch.

80 Risk mitigation through adapted loan products and lending procedures

Table 9: Loan features of short-term agricultural loans of interviewed MFIs

	CB				MFC		MBFI	
	Equity Bank		CRDB	Faulu		Juhudi Kilimo	Agaru SACCO	MC[2]
Name	General agric. loan for inputs, farm machinery, social needs	Farm input and equipment for grain and horticulture farmers	Micro-enterprises	General agric. loan for inputs, marketing, processing, animal husbandry, etc.	Agric. production loan for cereal farmer	Livestock loan for dairy farmers	General asset loan	General agric. production loan	General agric. loan (PAD)
Loan amount (in USD)[1]	11–1,140	11–1,140	57–5,700	40–6,000	n/a	n/a	114–342	Min. 20 (first loan: 20–80)	Max. 2,100
Loan term (months)	Max. 12	Max. 12	Max. 12	Max. 12	Max. 12	n/a	6–24 (average 12)	Max. 18	Max. 12 (24)[2]
Repayment schedule	Flexible; if possible interest monthly and principle as lump sum; grace period possible		Monthly interest, principle flexible; grace period possible	Monthly interest, principle flexible; grace period possible	Monthly interest, principle flexible; grace period possible	Flexible repayment; grace period possible	Grace period, then monthly repayment	Monthly interest, principle as balloon; grace period possible	Flexible, depends on activity; grace period possible
Collateral requirements	Household (hh) and farm assets; group loans: USD 4.5 cash collateral as group	Hh and farm assets, salary, cash cover	Guarantors, chattels, title deeds, log books, cash cover, debentures	Land titles, unregistered land, moveable assets (e.g. animals, hh property), personal guarantors	10% (first loan) or 20% (second loan) cash collateral		15% cash collateral; asset is collateral	Hh or farm assets	Joint liability or asset or cash collateral
Joint liability	Possible	Possible	n/a	n/a	Possible	Possible	Only	Possible	Possible
Other features	Partial disbursements; early repayment without penalty interest; credit life insurance	Direct payment to input dealer; credit life insurance	n/a	Partial disbursements	Crops and livestock insurance; life insurance; (livestock) farming as a business training; group loans: interest discount for early repayment		Partial disbursement; technical assistance visits, business training, loan insurance, life insurance (optional)	Own contribution (e.g. opening land); partial disbursement; loan protection fund	20% cash or in kind, contribution; loan insurance
Quoted i (p.a.)	15%	10%	15%	46% (28% after three loans)	20%	14–20%	32%	18%	12%

[1] All loans were offered in local currency but converted to USD to be comparable. Average exchange rates from June to September 2011, when interviews were conducted, were taken for conversion.
[2] The loan was designed under the PAD programme to have a loan term of 12 months. MC's have, however, the possibility to offer the loan also at a max. loan period of 24 months.

Source: own table based on interviews with MFIs and MFI websites.

Table 10: Loan features of medium-/long-term agricultural loans of interviewed MFIs

	CB			CRDB	MFC Juhudi Kilimo	Agaru SACCO		MBFI	CLCAM (Pehunco, Kouandé)
	Equity Bank								
Name	Commercial agric. (input and equipment)	Farm development	Modern agric. equipment	Animal traction	Microleasing	Assets for dairy value chain	Animal traction	Tractor loan	General agric. production and equipment loan	COMPACI loan
Loan amount[1] (in USD)	above 1,140	570–5,700	Above 342	40–800	40–400,000	342–3,420	Min. 20	Min. 20	No minimum or maximum loan amount	
Loan term (months)	Max. 36	Max. 24	Max. 24	Max. 24	Max. 60	12–24	Max. 24	Max. 36	Max. 24	Max. 24
Repayment schedule	Negotiated to match seasonality	n/a	n/a	Flexible, grace period on case-by-case basis	Flexible, grace period on case by case basis	Grace period, then monthly repayment	Interest monthly, principle flexible	n/a	n/a	Grace period; total repayment after cotton harvest
Collateral requirements	Depending on loan amount: e.g. logbooks, quoted shares, cash cover, title deeds	Depending on loan amount: personal guarantors, chattels (valuable hh items, machinery, animals), title deeds, logbooks, shares, cash cover, debentures		Purchased asset, land, machinery, equipment, or valuable hh items	Asset is collateral (CRDB keeps ownership until full repayment)	Purchased asset; 15% cash collateral, solidarity group	USD 80 cash collateral; hh or farm assets; joint liability possible	n/a	20% cash collateral; joint liability; individual loans: hh property and two personal guarantors	10% cash collateral; joint liability; loans above USD 1,000: additional guarantee
Other features	Credit life insurance	Credit life insurance	Credit life insurance; 20% cash contribution	In-kind loan	Insurance for leased asset; early repayment without penalty; automatic ownership after repayment; payment of risk factor; cash contribution	Business training; technical assistance visits; credit insurance; cow insurance, optional life insurance	Loan protection fund	Loan protection fund; 10% cash contribution	Loans above USD 440: collateral with value of twice the loan amount necessary; Life insurance	Repayment collection through AIC; equipment as in kind loan; life insurance
Quoted i (p.a.)	18% (red.)	17% (flat)	10% (flat)	25% (red.)	18.96% (red.)	32% (red.)	18% (red.)	18% (red.)	24%	12%

[1] All loans were offered in local currency but converted to USD to be comparable. Average exchange rates from June to September 2011, when interviews were conducted, were taken for conversion.

Source: own table based on interviews with MFIs and MFI websites.

Loan amount

The typically small loan size in traditional microfinance reflects the low debt capacity of borrowers. It can also serve as an indicator for the intended poverty outreach and/or the entry barrier of the respective MFI, as poorer clients can usually only borrow smaller amounts. (Ledgerwood 1999, 134)

The interviewed MFIs generally show very low entry barriers, especially for short-term working capital loans—the highest minimum working capital loan amount was USD 40 at CRDB. Only Juhudi Kilimo's minimum loan amount of USD 114 was much higher, which can be explained by their focus on asset financing. Medium-/long-term loans show a more diverse picture: whereas some MFIs offered very low minimum loan amounts (USD 20–40), Equity Bank's minimum medium-/long-term loan amounts were comparatively high (>USD 342); the "commercial agriculture" loan (loan amount >USD 1,140), in particular, seems to target wealthier farmers.

MC^2s applied a maximum loan amount of USD 2,100 to make sure that these specific loans (at lower interest rate than their other loans) were solely taken by smallholder farmers, as they assumed that larger farmers would need higher loan amounts (UGP/ADAF s.a.).

Loan term and repayment frequency

Chapter 4 illustrated that short loan terms and frequent repayments installments lead to two major difficulties for smallholder farmers, even though they are important risk management tools for MFIs in the absence of physical collateral.[71] First, microloans with short loan terms cannot be used to acquire larger assets (e.g. traction animals, irrigation pump) or invest in perennial crops as these investments would probably take more than a year to pay back (Christen/Pearce 2005, 36). Secondly, Figure 2 in Chapter 4 illustrated why loan terms and repayment schedules need to suit the cyclical cash flow of agricultural activities of smallholder farmers. It was shown that smallholders are prone to default under two circumstances: (1) if

---

[71] As a reminder: They shall: (1) allow closer monitoring and create an early warning system for the bank; (2) are considered essential to maintain financial discipline of the client, because regular meetings serve as a reminder and the personal relationship that can be established when loan officer and client regularly meet face to face support the feeling of responsibility towards the MFI; (3) early installments attract clients with incomes beside the financed investment, who are thus more likely to be able to repay even when the investment fails; and (4) the MFI can reuse the money faster for other clients, making the lending business for the MFI more profitable.

they have to meet regular repayments of the loan principle before they are able to earn their agricultural revenue, which often comes in one lump sum; and (2) if the loan term exceeds the agricultural cycle and smallholders have to repay long after they earned their agricultural income (e.g. when a farmers can harvest after 6 months but the loan term is 12 months, s/he will probably have spent the money for other purposes by time of repayment).

The interviewed MFIs addressed both challenges: most of them offered (some of their) loans at loan terms above 12 months and all offered flexible repayment schedules to adapt repayment installments to the respective agricultural activity and cash flow of a smallholder household. There are, however, some particularities.

One can mainly see two different approaches with regard to *loan terms*. The two CBs as well as Agaru SACCO offered several loan products at different loan terms, for example, a general agricultural loan with short loan term of a maximum of 12 months (18 months at Agaru SACCO) as well as a medium-term loan of up to 36 months to purchase traction animal or agricultural equipment. Besides having different loan terms, these loans also differ in their other loan features (e.g. interest rates, collateral requirements). CLCAMs and MC²s on the other hand only offered one general agricultural loan with a loan period of a maximum of 24–36 months. Their actual loan term was then based on the intended loan purpose and repayment capacity of the farmer. Many of their general agricultural loans thus also had a loan period of just one-crop cycle. While they were more flexible regarding their maximum loan period (e.g. they could also finance working capital with a loan period of 14 months), their loan features were less adapted to the specific risk (they did not, for example, charge different interest rates for different loan terms or change their collateral requirements, etc.).

It is also interesting to note that the loan term partly determines the agricultural activities a smallholder can finance through a loan (e.g. what kind of crop can be grown or which animals can be raised with support of a loan). Short-term loans of up to 12 months can be used to finance working capital for annual crops as well as some animal breeding. When asked about their short-term agricultural loans that also aim to finance animal husbandry, dairy farming, and agricultural equipment, Equity Bank, Faulu, and Juhudi Kilimo stated that a 12-month loan term is sufficient. They reported that an investment to purchase a cow can be repaid in 12 months due to the regular income from milk sales; rearing boilers have a cycle of

84 Risk mitigation through adapted loan products and lending procedures

around 2 months and vegetable farming in greenhouses allows several harvests a year.[72] Financing perennial crops or other animals with a short-term loan can, however, be difficult. Tree and bush crops require large upfront investments and entail a substantial wait before starting to fully produce (Christen/Pearce 2005, 36). Agaru SACCO also reported that they stopped financing sheep, goats, and swine, as these loans were not performing well when given out under an 18-months loan term due to the short repayment period.[73]

All MFIs had flexible **repayment schedules** that were able to meet the seasonality of agricultural activities. The repayment of the (bigger part of the) principle was adapted to the income flow from the respective agricultural activities, for example, for crop farmers after the harvest. Most MFIs, however, realized during their market research and/or their interaction with smallholder farmers that most smallholders have a diversified household income.[74] They grow different crops, have some livestock and are involved in some small off-farm businesses:

> "People are not just wheat farmers or maize farmers, but they are also dairy farmers, they do some horticulture farming, they have chicken or a goat. They do other things. And through this we realized, that the farmers can pay small amounts of the loan before the harvest /in course of the period and not just pay everything in bulk at the end."[75]

Most interviewed MFIs, therefore, treated the farming households as a unit, which means that they assessed the debt capacity and structured the loan repayments based on the overall cash flow of the household rather than on the prospective income from the agricultural activity of the investment. Interviewed MFIs often found that smallholder were able to repay a small part of the loan on a regular basis (e.g. the interest or the interest plus some part of the principle) and the bigger part in one lump sum at the end of the agricultural cycle (e.g. harvest). These findings are supported by Christen/Pearce (2005, 18), who state that "successful rural lenders recognize that farming households have multiple sources of income and therefore multiple sources for loan repayment".

---

[72] Relationship Officer for Agriculture, Equity Bank, Kikuyu branch; Consultant for Performance Management, Juhudi Kilimo; Agribusiness Development Manager, Faulu.
[73] Branch Manager, Agaru SACCO, Pader branch.
[74] Smallholder farmers diversify their household income to mitigate their own income risks that can occur due to weather extremes, plant pests, market price shocks, etc. (Doran et al. 2009, 11).
[75] Agribusiness Development Manager, Faulu.

The interviewed MFIs stated that treating the household as a unit, structuring loan repayment based on the overall household income and, therefore, having some (small) regular repayment installments from farmers offers much of the risk mitigation that traditional microfinance aims to achieve through regular loan repayments.[76] First, smallholders are regularly reminded of their loan, which maintains their financial discipline; secondly, smallholders realize that they have to repay the loan even in case their agricultural project fails; thirdly, all household members have to agree to help repay the loan, since the whole household income is taken into account; and fourthly, in case of an external event that destroys (part of) the crop, such as a heavy rain or severe dryness, smallholders are not left with the burden of the entire loan amount, but have already repaid some parts of it. The latter, however, is only true when regular repayments not only included interest repayments, but also part of the loan principle.

A regular repayment of loan principle in traditional microfinance has, however, two more aims that regular interest repayment cannot fulfil. First, regular repayments are used in traditional microfinance as an indicator for the well-being of the micro-business, as it can then be anticipated that the business will generate enough revenue to meet the regular installments. Hence, regular repayments reduce monitoring costs as loan officers only have to check on the respective client if installments are overdue. Secondly, regular repayments allow the MFI to reuse the money faster for other clients. Regular interest repayments cannot fulfil these functions, as they are too small to be significant for on-lending. Additionally, regular interest repayments do not allow any conclusions to be drawn regarding the well-being of the farming activity, since these small installments are met with other household incomes. Whether a farmer is performing well, for example, uses good agricultural practices and uses the loan money for the intended purpose or not, can therefore only be verified by a loan officer visiting the farm. In the words of the Agribusiness Development Manager at Faulu, "you may not know what is happening in the farm until you go physically there". In agricultural lending, loan officers have to physically go to the borrower, if they want to monitor the loan use as well as the well-being of the financed agricultural activity. This makes agricultural lending to smallholder farmers more expensive than lending to micro-enterprises. Costs are also enhanced because the assessment of the whole household cash flow, which

---

[76] Agribusiness General Manager, Equity Bank; Agricultural Product Specialist, RUCREF; Agribusiness Development Manager, Faulu.

is needed to structure the repayment rates, takes some time and requires a well-trained loan officer with thorough agricultural knowledge.

Collateral requirements
For the interviewed MFIs, collateral requirements for short-term agricultural loans were similar to the collateral requirements for traditional microloans. In most cases, they required a combination of joint group liability, non-traditional securities, cash collateral, and sometimes personal guarantors. Group lending will be further elaborated on in Section 7.2, as it also fulfils a range of purposes during loan assessment and monitoring. Collateral requirements for medium-/long-term loans depended on the loan size. The higher the loan, the more emphasis was placed on traditional collateral, such as quoted shares, cash collateral, or logbooks. When loans financed the purchase of assets, the asset was taken as collateral. Juhudi Kilimo even applied ear tags with their company logo to the cows financed through their loans and the bank remained owner of the purchased asset until it was fully paid under CRDB's microleasing product.[77]

Non-traditional securities include household or farm items that are of value for the smallholder. These can be motorcycles, chicken, television, etc. Equity Bank even takes a tree as collateral as long as the tree is important for the farmer. Even if most of these items do not have a high monetary value for the MFI in case of default (because it is mostly too expensive and time consuming to sell them), the fact that the MFI is entitled to take the item away from the farmer in case of default is generally a sufficient incentive to repay.[78]

Many of the interviewed MFIs also required some **cash collateral** from smallholders. Farmers had to save a certain percentage of the loan amount in advance and deposit it in a bank account until the whole loan was repaid. Besides serving as cash collateral, the process of saving upfront was quoted as having some value in itself.[79] The process of saving money, which often takes farmers some time, demonstrates the smallholders' commitment and teaches them some financial discipline. Some of the interviewed MFIs also used this time for regular group meetings to build trust, teach farmers basic financial management, and allow the

---

[77] Consultant for Performance Management, Juhudi Kilimo; CRDB 2013b.
[78] Agribusiness General Manager, Equity Bank; Kyanika Nsibambi 2010, 46ff.; Head of Accounting and Control of Micro Bank Department, ADAF.
[79] Agribusiness General Manager, Equity Bank; Consultant for Performance Management, Juhudi Kilimo Agaru SACCO.

group to mature.[80] According to Equity Bank, the amount of the (group) savings is not as important as the whole process itself, which takes around 6–8 weeks. During this time of weekly meetings, smallholder groups save

> "maybe around 100 Ksh [USD 1] per meeting, per week. That is about 400 Ksh per month. This also forms part of the collateral for the loan. And when they know, they have some savings somewhere with you; they want to repay their loans, so that their money is still safe in the bank. So we give them time to know each other, to train them and (...) they also feel that they are ready to take up the loan."[81]

Meetings are also attended by a loan officer of Equity Bank who interacts with farmers, builds a relationship, and has the chance to get to know the smallholders, their financial discipline and their (agricultural) activities.

Personal guarantors co-sign the loan agreement and have to repay the loan in case of default. They are often respected community leaders and "assist in monitoring the client and providing any useful information to the Bank in case of any problems which may affect loan repayments". (Kyanika Nsibambi 2010, 46ff.)

Agaru SACCO developed an interesting approach on how to use land without land titles as collateral for their loans. Land is not accepted as collateral by many MFIs either due to lack of land titles or political reluctance to enforce legal contracts and claim land in compensation for a non-repaid loan, as it would take away the basis of smallholders' livelihood (Christen/Pearce 2005, 38). In northern Uganda, where Agaru SACCO operates, abundant land is available. Smallholders can easily pledge some as collateral without fear of losing their means of livelihood. Land titles, however, do not exist and land is also often owned by the whole family or community and not individually. When Agaru SACCO first started agricultural lending, they would only accept proper land titles as collateral, but realized quickly that very few people were able to benefit from loans as a consequence. So

> "we [Agaru SACCO] decided to come back to the drawing board and found that we can lower ourselves down and even involve all family members, involve the clan members and consider their discussion as something vital that can be used as collateral security."[82]

Today their procedure is as follows. All family and community members, including a local council, discuss the situation when one of their community members wants

---

[80] Agribusiness General Manager, Equity Bank; Consultant for Performance Management, Juhudi Kilimo.
[81] Credit Officer for Agriculture, Equity Bank, Kikuyu branch.
[82] Loan Officer for Agriculture, Agaru SACCO, Kalongo branch.

88   Risk mitigation through adapted loan products and lending procedures

to pledge a piece of land as collateral. If they all agree on it, Agaru SACCO accepts the piece of land as collateral without requiring legal land titles.

> "We want all the minutes of that meeting and that meeting has to be attended by at least a local council, which is the one representing the government at local level. Then the family members all have to consent that we have given that land (number of acres, starting from this place to this place) - at least it has to be specified. Then if they have specified it, we take it as collateral security, because it is very expensive to process land titles. (...) At least we have decided to lower ourselves a little bit down to see that everyone can benefit as long as there is consensus from the family members here."[83]

Further loan features for risk mitigation

Interviewed MFIs also applied some additional loan features to their agricultural loans for smallholder farmers that were intended to mitigate credit risk.

Some interviewed MFIs released the loan money in **partial disbursements** aligned with the different agricultural production steps of a smallholder. If a smallholder wanted USD 50 of which s/he needed USD 20 for seeds, USD 20 for lending a tractor and USD 10 for hiring a worker, for example, the money would be needed at different times. If it is all given in one instalment, it is unrealistic that the money for the harvest worker will be saved over several weeks until the worker is to be paid.[84] It therefore reduces the MFI's risk to unblock the different installments when they are needed and under the condition that the previous agricultural production steps were successfully completed. If a loan officer finds that a smallholder only managed to plant half of the acreage compared to what s/he initially intended or that most of a chicken farmer's chicks died after hatching, for example, the MFI can withhold the next instalment or only disburse part of the next instalment. While this can greatly reduce the credit risk for an MFI, it requires regular monitoring by a loan officer who understands agriculture and is able to identify whether a crop or an animal is well cared for or not. Partial disbursements also help to reduce loan diversion:

> "For most of the loans, we do partial disbursements. Because I am not assured if I give you the money at planting that you reach harvest. And money, money is a big problem. Everybody wants to use the money they have and nobody will wait for harvesting time when they need the money [to pay harvest labour]"[85]

---

[83]   Loan Officer for Agriculture, Agaru SACCO, Kalongo branch.
[84]   Financial Development Consultant, aBi Trust.
[85]   Agribusiness General Manager, Equity Bank.

Christen/Pearce (2005, 32) also found that successful lenders applied staggered cash disbursements to meet production schedules.

Timing, however, is critical in agricultural production and the timely application of pesticides or fungicides in case of plant disease can be the difference of the success or failure of an entire crop. MFIs, therefore, need to know the production cycle and timing of the different agricultural activities they finance very well and they need to be up to date with the happenings in the field (e.g. the outbreak of a plant disease). Partial disbursements can also increase the transaction costs for smallholders, as they have to travel to the MFI branch for the collection of every disbursement. Depending on the distances and road infrastructure, this might be very time consuming and cost intensive. Mobile banking or agency banking (see Section 8.4) can dramatically reduce these costs for smallholders.

Link loans with insurance products
One or several compulsory insurance products were attached to most of the offered loan products of the interviewed MFIs. An obligatory credit life insurance (sometimes also called loan insurance or loan protection fund) was part of the majority of offered loan products, while some MFIs also insured the assets they financed or had a weather insurance product.

The credit life insurance was thought to release the family, joint liability group members, or the personal guarantors from the burden of repaying a loan in case of death of the borrower, while the MFIs still received the outstanding amount from the insurance company or the loan protection fund.[86] The insurance premium ranged from 0.6% to 2% to be paid as an upfront fee. Juhudi Kilimo and Faulu also insured all purchased cows of smallholders against death and illness and CRDB insured all leased assets under their microleasing scheme. Insuring these assets mitigates the credit risk for smallholders as well as for MFIs, as smallholders were re-funded in case of, for example, the death of a cow and were, therefore, still able to repay their loans. The threat of over-indebtedness due to external circumstances is mitigated through these types of insurances.

Since weather extremes are major risks for farmers involved in crop farming and also pose a high co-variant risk to MFIs, as they can destroy the crops of all farmers in a respective area, MFIs were interested in weather insurance products.

---

[86] While commercial banks cooperated with an insurance company, membership-based financial institutions mostly operated their own loan protection fund.

90 Risk mitigation through adapted loan products and lending procedures

These are, however, not yet broadly available in SSA due to several reasons. Generally, weather insurance can be offered through two approaches: (1) indemnity-based insurance (e.g. single-peril or multiple-peril insurance), under which the insurance payouts are based on the actual loss at the unit level; or (2) index-based insurance (e.g. weather index insurance), under which the insurance payouts are based on an index measurement (Iturrioz 2009, 6). Since indemnity-based insurance policies require field visits to assess the respective damage and income loss, they are not appropriate for individual smallholders, as the costs would far outweigh any damage.[87] Weather index insurances, on the other hand, are much cheaper, as they pay out based on the value of an index and not on losses measured in the field. Indexes are variables that are highly correlated with the losses, for example, rainfall or temperature, and that cannot be influenced by the insured. While weather index insurance could be used in the smallholder context, it is very difficult to set up the systems needed for a weather index insurance. Indexes are quite area specific, which is why a broad coverage area with weather stations (approx. one weather station every 20 km) is required as well as specific historical weather data to design the insurance product.[88] Despite these difficulties, two interviewed MFIs experimented with different weather insurance products: Equity Bank piloted a weather index insurance while Faulu offered a multiple-peril insurance product which was adapted to smallholder farmers.

Equity Bank started their weather index insurance pilots in 2010 in partnership with the insurance company "APA insurance" and with the support of other development partners. According to the Agribusiness General Manager of Equity Bank, they were

> "still experiencing challenges of data. We still don't have a reliable source of data dating 30 years back. So where we have, we go and pilot. We have done it in some areas, but not all the areas."[89]

Faulu was keen to develop weather insurance products, as they had experienced severe loan defaults due to heavy droughts in their first years of offering agricultur-

---

[87] Jubilee Insurance, a Kenyan insurance company involved in agricultural insurance, therefore, only offers multiple-peril insurance for farmers with more than 20 acres (Agricultural Insurance Expert, Jubilee Insurance).
[88] Agricultural Insurance Expert, Jubilee Insurance.
[89] Detailed information on the set-up and experiences with weather index insurance products in Kenya are documented by James Sina (2012).

al loans to smallholder farmers. They therefore started to cooperate with an insurance company to develop a weather insurance product for smallholder farmers in the absence of weather stations within their area of operation. Index-based insurance was, therefore, not an option for Faulu. At the time of the interviews they had just introduced a compulsory multiple-peril crop insurance, where the insurance company did not assess the loss of every single farmer in case of extreme weather events, but calculated an overall loss for a specific area:

> "You go to the area and assess the harvest in that area to see if there is 100% failure or 30%. Then they [insurance company] pay either the difference or total loss. (...) [Now] look at a farmer that borrowed 50,000 Ksh. In the course of the year they pay maybe 15,000 Ksh, the remaining is 35,000 Ksh. When there is a total failure of crop, the farmer still gets back the 50,000 Ksh from the insurance company. And then they can start again and also get a new loan immediately. So because they already paid back the interest rate, they even earn a little even though there is a total crop failure."[90]

So the combination of an insurance product together with monthly interest repayments is thought to secure the MFI from loan losses due to weather extremes and the smallholder from total income failure.

According to Equity Bank, Faulu, and Jubilee Insurance, insurance products need to be coupled to a loan product and to be made obligatory. First, most smallholders are not familiar with the concept of insurance and would not voluntarily pay for it, and secondly transaction costs of insurance products are still too high to offer them individually, which is why an insurance company can only offer these products in partnership with an MFI and when insurance products are made obligatory.[91]

Increasing loan amounts and declining interest rates
Increasing loan amounts and/or declining interest rates are also loan features that can be applied to offer repayment incentives and reduce credit risk. Agaru SACCO offered a maximum agricultural loan amount of USD 57 to first-time clients. Only after the borrower proves to perform well with this small loan amount can the amount of the following loan be increased. Agaru SACCO thereby reduces their credit risk to a maximum of USD 57 for first-time clients that they do not yet know well.

---

[90] Agribusiness Development Manager, Faulu.
[91] Agricultural Insurance Expert, Jubilee Insurance.

CRDB, on the other hand, charged agricultural first-time clients much higher interest rates then they charged their existing clients. While their interest rates were at 46% p.a. for the first three loans, they dropped to 28% afterwards.[92]

Own contribution

Most MFIs required some contribution of borrowers to the funded project, either in cash or in kind, for example, preparing the field for planting if the loan was taken for crop farming. They did so to keep the ownership with the farmer and ensure that s/he also has a stake in case the project fails:

> "If you fund the farmer a 100 %, first they even forget it's their farm, it looks more like the bank's farm. I mean you have funded everything, the farmer did not have any contribution."[93]

Cooperation with value chain actors

Cooperation with value chain actors can help to mitigate loan diversion and credit risk. While all interviewed MFIs claimed to have a value chain approach, only some MFIs incorporated the collaboration with value chain actors into their loan product design.

For their farm input and equipment loan for small-scale horticulture and grain farmers, Equity Bank collaborated with input dealers to avoid loan diversion. Smallholders do not receive cash to buy the inputs, but can pick inputs with a voucher from a recognized input dealer, who is then directly paid by Equity Bank.[94]

CLCAM's COMPACI loan had a similar approach for agricultural equipment. Once the farmer was granted a credit, the MFI requested the agricultural equipment at COBEMAG (the company producing the agricultural equipment) and paid them directly. The smallholder then received the equipment without handling cash in between. Loan repayments were not handled by the farmer himself either, but directly deducted from the farmers' cotton income after harvest. As all farmers in Benin were paid through the Association Interprofessionelle du Coton (AIC), the collaboration with AIC allowed the deduction of the loan repayment before payments were made to farmers. This extremely reduces the transaction costs and risks for an MFI.

---

[92] Loan Officer for Agriculture, CRDB, Lira branch.
[93] Agribusiness General Manager, Equity Bank.
[94] Agribusiness General Manager, Equity Bank.

Faulu also wanted to start cooperation with input dealers to avoid loan diversion and insure high-quality inputs for smallholders. At the time of the interview, they were in the process of building up this cooperation, but had not yet started paying directly to input dealers.

Mitigating market price risks through warehouse receipts
Highly fluctuating market prices pose high external risks to a farmer's income and thus the repayment of loans as described in Chapter 3. Some MFIs, therefore, started to offer warehouse receipts to mitigate this risk.

Market prices for agricultural products are often very low during harvest time due to the high supply of agricultural products. Combined with the often pressing cash need of smallholders, many farmers sell their products at very low prices. The logic behind warehouse receipt systems is that farmers bring their harvested crops to a licensed warehouse, where it is securely stored until it can be sold at higher prices. Farmers, who remain owners of their products, receive a receipt stating the quantity and quality of the stored product. They can now use this receipt as collateral for a loan. A lender would then generally give a specific percentage of the current value of the stored product as a loan to a farmer. In case of loan default, the lender can sell the products and is thus secured against loan default as well as against price changes. The farmer has the advantage of storing his/her product safely until market prices are at their peak or a better price can be achieved through bulking his/her products with other farmers. (Meyer 2011, 37ff.)

While two MFIs (Equity Bank and Faulu) collaborated with existing warehouses, Agaru SACCO was piloting its own warehouse, as there were not any warehouses within their region. Agaru SACCO itself managed the warehouse and was also responsible for bulking and selling the products. Agaru SACCO planned on handing over the management to existing farmers' organizations after the initial pilot phase. All MFIs were convinced of the importance of warehouses for farmers to achieve higher incomes, but they all also experienced some challenges. Equity Bank solely worked with the only private warehouse in the country. They decided not to work with the large number of public/governmental warehouses, because the governmental warehouses had management problems and reliability was an issue, for example, a client could receive three receipts for the same bag of maize, which poses a problem for MFIs. Additionally, it is very important that the quantity and quality of the agricultural products is well measured so that the value of the product and thus the loan amount can be determined.[95] Moreover, the product has to be properly stored to prevent spoiling or a loss of quality. Agaru SACCO struggled also with these problems of measuring quality and quantity and storing the produce correctly (at right temperature and moisture).[96]

Another challenge of warehouses is their accessibility for smallholder farmers. If warehouses are too far away and/or local collection points are missing, smallholders might still sell their products at low prices to middlemen who would then use the warehouse storage facilities. In this scenario, better prices and warehouse receipts would not reach smallholders.

7.1.2 Discussion of interest rates

As outlined in Section 4.1, there is a controversy surrounding interest rates for agricultural loans for smallholder farmers. While there is a strong need for MFIs to be financially viable and, therefore, charge cost covering interest rates, some people question whether smallholder farmers can afford to pay these interest rates. This challenge is exacerbated by the fact that lending to smallholder farmers includes higher transaction costs and risks, which also have to be covered by MFIs. There is no easy answer to the question on "adequate" interest rates for smallholder farmers, as it will greatly depend on the country context, the respective farmers, and the agricultural activity. The topic is, however, too important to be left out (as is the case in almost all reviewed studies).[97] The following section will, therefore, shed some light on different aspects. First, it will compare the quoted interest rates of microcredits for small entrepreneurs with the interest rates for agricultural micro-credits at the same MFI. In theory, agricultural microloans should have a higher interest rate to cover the additional risks and costs. This was, however, not the case for all interviewed MFIs. The respective paragraph will, therefore, also explore how MFIs covered the additional costs of agricultural lending. Secondly, the EIRs for the offered agricultural loans for smallholder farmers will be calculated to know the real costs farmers have to bear when taking a micro-loan. Thirdly, the effects of different interest rates on an "average" smallholder cotton farmer will be assessed by drawing on the experiences of COMPACI. COMPACI collected data on smallholder cotton farmers over a period of more than 6 years and from six different coun-

---
[95] Agribusiness General Manager, Equity Bank.
[96] Branch Manager, Agaru SACCO, Pader branch.
[97] Only Harper (2005 and 2008) was found to approach this issue.

tries. By drawing on this data it is possible to compare the effect on yields and income through the use of inputs and calculate whether or not it is worth buying these inputs on credit and how this decision is influenced by the level of interest rates.

It is important to bear in mind that all quoted interest rates of the interviewed MFIs are from the summer of 2011. Since interest rates are a function of the above-named aspects, they are prone to change to adjust for changing market interest rates, inflation rates, changing costs structures, etc.

Comparison of interest rates—agriculture vs. commerce
While most MFIs felt that agricultural lending for smallholder farmers implies higher transaction costs than lending to micro-entrepreneurs due to longer distances to reach farmers and intensive monitoring as well as acquiring adequate agricultural know-how, their risk perception regarding smallholder lending differed. Some MFIs perceived agricultural microfinance to be riskier due to fact that they experienced lower repayment rates from smallholders than from small entrepreneurs.[98] Other MFIs did not support this notion and claimed that credit risks for agricultural lending to smallholder farmers can be mitigated if one knows the agricultural smallholder sector well.[99] These different perceptions are not mirrored in the level of interest rates, however. Most MFIs did not charge higher interest rates for agricultural loans than for their other microloans as can be seen in Table 11. Quite the contrary, some MFIs even charged lower or equal interest rates for agricultural loans compared to their other microloans. Only two MFIs (CRDB, Faulu) charged higher interest rates for agricultural loans. Additional costs of agricultural lending could, however, also be covered through additional fees and charges instead of charging higher quoted interest rates. This cannot be examined, because fees and charges for traditional microloans were not recorded during the interviews.

---

[98] Loan Officer for Agriculture, CRDB, Lira branch; Agricultural Product Specialist, RUCREF; Executive Secretary, ADAF.
[99] Agribusiness General Manager, Equity Bank; Credit Officer for Agriculture, Equity Bank, Kikuyu branch; Loan Officer for Agriculture, CRDB, Lira branch.

96 Risk mitigation through adapted loan products and lending procedures

Table 11: Comparison of interest rates of agricultural and commercial loans

		CB		MFC			MBFI		
		Equity Bank	CRDB	Faulu	Juhudi Kilimo	Agaru SACCO	CLCAM (Pehunco, Kouandé)		MC²
							CLCAM	COMPACI	PAD
Agric.	Short-term i (%)	10–15	46 (28)	20	32	18	24	12	≤12
	Medium-/long-term i (%)	10–18	25	n/a	32	18	24	12	≤12
Commercial i (%)		18	22	15	n/a¹	36	24	24	12–18
Agric. i higher/lower than commercial i		Lower	Higher	Higher	n/a	Lower	Same	Lower	Lower/same

¹ Juhudi Kilimo only offers agricultural loans.
Source: own table based on interviews with MFIs.

MFIs had different explanations for their approach regarding interest rates. MFIs charging higher interest rates for agricultural loans justified these with higher transaction costs and their striving for financial viability:

> "And also, agricultural lending is expensive. If you count the cost of transport and monitoring, if you count the cost of advertising for the market information for me to be able to know how the prices are changing, if you put all that, you put that at variable costs, it is expensive, it is hell expensive."[100]

Lump sum payments at the end of the agricultural cycle were also stated to imply higher costs, as the money cannot be used for giving out new loans during the loan period.[101] While Faulu, which charged higher interest rates for agriculture, aimed at reducing these rates as high interest rates were perceived to create problems for smallholders, CRDB experienced that smallholders were capable of earning high profits and bearing the costs of interest rates as high as 46% through their agricultural activities without difficulties.[102]

MFIs charging lower interest rates for agricultural loans than commercial micro-loans had a different perception of the topic. They stated that agricultural rates of return are lower than rates of return for small trade or commercial activities in most cases and, therefore, found that smallholders needed lower interest rates:

---

[100] Agricultural Product Specialist, RUCREF.
[101] Agribusiness Development Manager, Faulu.
[102] Agribusiness Development Manager, Faulu; Loan Officer for Agriculture, CRDB, Lira branch.

"And we all know that the agricultural sector, when you look at the internal rate of returns, is lower than business. Ok, I want to grow maize. What kind of maize can I really grow to be able to pay that 5 % per month? It's almost impossible, because the internal rate of return most of the time is 20 % to 22 %, you see. And you have to cover all your charges and so on, before paying the interest rate."[103]

These MFIs addressed the challenge of high transaction costs through other means than charging higher interest rates. Equity Bank's approach was to realize high volumes on the number of loans, for example, through meeting groups of smallholders for loan appraisals and monitoring instead of meeting individuals:

"We realize that those who are doing agriculture, there are so many of them. So we have the low margin - high volume advantage. You may make small amounts from so many people. So then you still have a profit, that business is still viable."[104]

Equity Bank also cooperated with external agents to lower their interest rates for some loans. Their grain and horticultural loan for smallholders was implemented in cooperation with the Alliance for a Green Revolution (AGRA), the International Fund for Agricultural Development (IFAD), the government of Kenya and Amiran Kenya. These partners helped reduce costs and risks by setting up a loan guarantee fund and offering technical assistance. Additionally, the MoA helped administer the credits and input loans were directly paid to reputable agro input dealers to avoid loan diversion by farmers (IBLF 2013; Equity Bank 2013b). ADAF also used group lending to reduce outreach costs and received governmental funds to support their agricultural lending activities within the PAD-MC² programme. These funds were used for technical support, for example, the purchase of motorcycles to be able to make farm visits, training of loan officers and development of simple agronomic indicators that can be used during loan assessment. Additionally, MC²s were granted a revolving fund for on-lending to smallholder farmers at a maximum interest rate of 12% p.a. Some MC²s also decided to generally cross-subsidize their agricultural loans through their other loan products, because they felt the importance of the agricultural sector for the community and the need to support smallholders. The Executive Secretary of ADAF described the reasons for this decision as follows:

---

[103] Executive Secretary, ADAF.
[104] Relationship Officer for Agriculture, Equity Bank, Kikuyu branch.

98   Risk mitigation through adapted loan products and lending procedures

"Il y a un qui fait le commerce, il y a différentes activités et (…) c'est une coopérative, c'est une association. Il y a la solidarité. Ca veut dire que là où on gagne un peut d'argent, ca peut permettre supporter l'autre parti. Parce que moi, le producteur agricole, je produis, je ne gagne pas grand chose, mais je vends au commerçants. Le commerçant lui il gagne beaucoup. Il faut un système de compensation. (…) parce que si l'autre ne produit plus, aussi le commerçant ne va rien avoir. Celui qui vend le savon dans la boutique, il est producteur n'a pas d'argent, il ne va pas venir acheter le savon. Donc c'est un système."[105]

CLCAMs, on the other hand, were able to offer lower interest rates for their COMPACI loan, as they were able to outsource some part of their loan monitoring and repayment collection to other value chain actors and thereby greatly reduced their own costs. Agricultural extension officers helped in monitoring the cotton smallholder during their general extension work and AIC, which paid cotton smallholders after the cotton harvest, deducted the loan amounts before paying the farmer. Unfortunately, the above-described mechanism experienced some difficulties during its first 2 years, in which AIC did not deduct the loan as planned before paying the farmers. CLCAMs, therefore, had to "run after the money"[106] themselves and suffered some losses as the interest rate of 12% could not cover the high costs for repayment collection. At the time of the interview CLCAMs were, therefore, not sure whether they would still offer the COMPACI loan at 12% for the next year, but rather opted to offer their general agricultural loan at 24%, which was able to cover all related transaction costs.

EIRs—the real costs for smallholder farmers
In addition to their quoted interest rate, MFIs require different fees and charges from borrowers, for example, loan application fees, compulsory (life) insurance, commitment fees, etc. Interest rates were also calculated using different methods: the reducing loan balance method calculates interest based on the outstanding loan amount over the loan term (which is declining with regular repayments), whereas the flat method calculates interest as a percentage of the initial loan amount.[107] The EIR includes all these financial costs of a loan and thus shows the true costs of borrowing for clients and the potential revenue earned by MFIs (Ledgerwood 1999, 140ff.).

---

[105]   Executive Secretary, ADAF.
[106]   General Manager, CLCAM Pehunco.
[107]   A detailed description of the two calculation methods as well as examples for their effect on actual costs of loans can be found in Ledgerwood (1999, 140ff.).

The calculation of the EIRs for different loans offered by the interviewed MFIs was conducted with the MicroFinance Transparency (2012) interest calculation tool and is shown in Tables 12 and 13. Although fees and charges such as insurance, cash collateral, commitment, and application fees were taken into account, costs for opening or having an account (e.g. account maintenance charges, withdrawing charges, minimum account balances) and interest on savings were not taken into account, even though these elements also influence the EIR.[108] The assessment of these aspects was not possible as most MFIs had several accounts (individual, group, current, savings, etc.) with different fee structures. All fees and charges of the different MFIs taken for the calculation of EIRs in Tables 12 and 13 are listed in Annex C.

Tables 12 and 13 both depict the general agricultural loans of CLCAMs and MC²s. Their general agricultural loan has a maximum loan period of 24 months and can, therefore, be taken for short-term working capital such as inputs, but also to purchase equipment which will be repaid within the medium term of 24 months. As the EIR is greatly influenced by the loan period, both calculations were made.

Table 12: Short-term loans—effective vs. quoted interest rate

	CB			MFC			MBFI		
	Equity Bank			CRDB	Faulu	Juhudi Kilimo	Agaru SACCO	CLCAM (Pehunco, Kouandé)	MC²
Loan	Farm input	Grain and hortic. small	Micro-enter-prises	Agric. loan	Cereal farmers loan	Asset finance loans	Agric. loan	Agric. loan	COMPACI loan	Agric. loan (PAD)
Quoted i (% p.a.)	15	10	15	46 (28)¹	20	32²	18	24	12	≤12³
EIR (% p.a.)	24–28	18–21	24–28	63–68	31–37	57–59	28–36	39–41	17–19	16–18
PTI (%)	61–68	51–59	61–68	87–92	63–73	61–66	58–72	68–72	68–75	71–83

¹ After three loans, interest rate is reduced to 28%.
² Calculated on reducing balance, 2 months grace period and with equal monthly installments.
³ Quoted interest rate of PAD loan always has to be 12% or lower.

Source: own table based on interviews with MFIs, fees and charges for CRDB and Juhudi Kilimo taken from MicroFinance Transparency (2013a and 2013b); EIR and PTI calculated with MicroFinance Transparency (2012).

---

[108] Considering interest on savings would reduce the EIR, whereas account opening and maintenance fees would increase the EIR.

100   Risk mitigation through adapted loan products and lending procedures

Table 13:   Medium-/long-term loans—effective vs. quoted interest rate

	CB			MFC		MBFI					
	Equity Bank			CRDB		Juhudi Kilimo	Agaru SAC-CO		CLCAM (Pehunco, Kouandé)		MC²
Loan	Agric. commercial	Farm development	Agric. equipment	Animal traction	Microleasing	Dairy farming	Animal traction	Trac-tor	Agric. loan	COMPACI	Agric. loan (PAD)	
Quoted i (% p.a.)	18 (red.)	17 (flat)	10 (flat)	25 (red.)	18.96 (red.)	32 (red.)	18 (red.)	18 (red.)	24 (red.)	12 (red.)	≤12 (red.)¹	≤12 (flat)¹
EIR (% p.a.)	22–23	30–31	19	31–32	33–36	56–58	36–37	23–25	38	16	15	21–22
PTI (%)	83–85	59–60	54	85–87	62–75	62–64	53–54	75–83	68–69	79	82–85	58–59

¹ Approx. 70% of all MC²s have reducing interest rates while the rest has flat interest rates. Both calculations were therefore made.

Source: own table based on interviews with MFIs; EIR and PTI calculated with MicroFinance Transparency (2012).

Tables 12 and 13 present the EIR as a range, because it is influenced by the lending period. For short-term loans, the EIR was calculated for a 6-month and a 12-month loan period with monthly interest rate payments and a lump sum principle payment at the end of the loan term. In this case, it makes no difference whether or not the reducing or the flat calculation method is used.[109] For the medium-/long-term loans the EIR was calculated for most loans with a loan period of 18 months and 24 months, as the maximum loan period with most MFIs was 24 months. Exceptions were Agaru SACCO's tractor loan with a maximum loan period of 36 months and CRDB's microleasing with a lending period of up to 60 months, for which these longer loan terms were also taken for EIR calculation. To compare the different medium-/long-term loan products, the EIR was calculated with a partial repayment of principle and interest every 6 months, even though repayments rates are flexible in reality and thus depend on the crop cycle. Due to the partial repayment of principle every 6 months, using the declining or the flat method results in a big difference.

The Pricing Transparency Index (PTI) is a tool of the MicroFinance Transparency organization and calculates the percentage of the loan price that is communicated by the lender's quoted interest rate to the borrower. Thus, a PIT of 100% would be a perfectly transparent loan pricing. MicroFinance Transparency rates an index between 80% and 100% as "good" (MicroFinance Transparency 2013c, 1).

---

[109]   The calculation was only different for the EIR of Juhudi Kilimo, since Juhudi Kilimo only offers regular repayments that start after 2 months. Thus the EIR was calculated with a loan period of 6 and 12 months, regular repayments of principle and interest on declining balance and a grace period of 2 months.

There are two interesting observations to be made from Tables 12 and 13:
(1) EIRs as well as quoted interest rates differ significantly between the different MFIs. While the quoted interest rates range from 10% to 46% p.a. across short- and medium-/long-term loans, the EIR ranges from 15% up to 68% p.a. Even the interest rates of MFIs operating in the same country (e.g. CRDB and Agaru SACCO in Uganda as well as Equity Bank, Juhudi Kilimo, and Faulu in Kenya) vary considerably, from 18% to 46% p.a. (quoted interest rate) or 28–68% p.a. (EIR) in Uganda and 10–32% p.a. (quoted interest rate) or 22–59% p.a. (EIR) in Kenya. Drawing general conclusions seems difficult considering this wide range. It seems, however, that charging EIRs well below 20% p.a. for smallholder farmers seems difficult, as all loans with quoted interest rates below 12% p.a. and EIRs below 21% p.a. received external support aimed among others at lowering the interest rate. This is the case for Equity's grain and horticultural loan for smallholders, CLCAMs' COMPACI loan for cotton farmers and the PAD agricultural loans of MC²s.[110]

(2) Most loans show a significant deviation between quoted interest rates and EIR. Only a total of six loans out of 22 achieve a transparency rating above 80% and could, therefore, be rated as "good", that is, "transparent". Most agricultural loans for smallholders are thus not very transparent and smallholders might pay much more for their loans than they know. Calculating loans with reducing compared to flat interest rates, in particular, results in quite a large difference for medium-/long-term loans and/or loans with regular repayments, which is illustrated through MC²s agricultural loan. The EIR is at 15% p.a. when calculated with the reducing balance method and at 22% p.a. when calculated with the flat method using the same quoted interest rate and the same fees and charges. Looking at fees and charges as well as the calculation method (flat or declining) is, therefore, of great importance when designing loan products for smallholders. For this reason, external factors that may become engaged with the goal of reducing interest rates for smallholders should focus on the EIR rather than on the quoted interest rate. Additionally, more transparent pricing could help borrowers know the true cost of borrowing and prevent them from becoming over indebted or finding themselves facing repayment difficulties.

---

[110] Only Equity's modern agricultural equipment loan also falls below this line and it is not clear whether it also received any kind of external support.

Effect of interest rates on a smallholder cotton farmer in SSA

Seeing the different levels of EIRs for agricultural loans (ranging from 15% to 68% p.a.) and knowing that some MFIs charge lower and others higher interest rates for agricultural loans than for their other microloans, the question on the actual effect of these different interest rates on smallholders arises. Are smallholders profitable enough to generate sufficient revenues through agricultural investments to meet all these different levels of interest rates or can they only afford interest rates below a specific level? And is the level of interest rate relevant at all for smallholders considering all the other factors influencing the productivity and profitability of smallholders (such as highly varying farm gate prices, changing input prices, etc.)? These questions are especially relevant since governments continue to discuss interest rates ceilings for agricultural loans and development organizations and/or donors channel much money into loan guarantee funds and other activities to lower interest rates for smallholders. The following paragraphs will, therefore, elaborate on these questions by drawing on data from COMPACI. COMPACI is only present in one of the countries, in which interviews were conducted (Benin). However, since it provides profound data on cotton farmers from six different African countries (Zambia, Malawi, Mozambique, Côte d'Ivoire, Burkina Faso, and Benin) that are generally not publicly available, the paper will draw on COMPACI numbers for the following calculations.

To assess the influence of different interest rates as compared to varying farm gate prices on smallholder cotton farmer's income, a calculation will be made based on COMPACI project data on the average cotton productivity of smallholder farmers using chemical fertilizers vs. smallholders not using chemical fertilizers and the additional investment associated with these inputs (Table 14). Higher cotton production is highly dependent on expensive (chemical) fertilizers. Due to the higher productivity but also due to more weeds that grow through the use of fertilizer, labour increases and workers have to be hired to help in the cotton fields. The additional cost of hired labour, therefore, often comes with the use of fertilizer. The costs for chemicals also increase (e.g. for herbicides). Table 14 shows that a smallholder is able to produce 500 kg/ha more at additional costs of USD 158 on average.[111]

---

[111] Figures are averages. Detailed figures on seed cotton productivity in respective countries as well as input costs and farmer's net revenue can be found in Peltzer/Röttger 2013, 14ff.

Table 14: Costs of cotton production in SSA

Indicator	Cotton production without fertilizer[1]	Cotton production with fertilizer[2]
Cotton seeds (USD/ha)	8	8
Chemicals (USD/ha)	32	50
Chemical fertilizer (USD/ha)	-	125
Hired labour for 20 days (USD/ha)	-	15
Total costs (USD/ha)	**40**	**198**
Productivity (kg/ha)	600	1,100
Additional productivity (kg/ha)	500	
Additional cost of production (USD/ha)	158	

[1] Numbers are averages based on COMPACI data from Zambia and Malawi.
[2] Number are averages based on COMPACI data from Côte d'Ivoire and Burkina Faso.
Source: own table based on internal COMPACI project reports.

For the following calculation, it is assumed that the smallholders finance the entire additional investment through a loan from an MFI. The additional income of a farmer is, therefore, a function of the additional productivity through the use of inputs multiplied with the farm gate price (additional revenue) minus the additional expenses, that is, the additional costs of production (taken as loan) as well as the interest rate payments on the loan (see Formula 1). The period for an input credit for cotton is usually 6 months and the loan principle is repaid in one lump sum after the cotton harvest, while the interest is paid monthly. Compounded interest rates effects are, therefore, not included in the following calculation. The annual interest rate is divided by two in Formula 1 to derive at the interest paid for 6 months.

ΔI = Additional income (USD)
p = Additional productivity (kg/ha) = 500 kg/ha
fgp = Farm gate price (USD/kg)
cp = Additional cost of production (USD/ha) = 158 USD/ha
i = Interest rate p.a.

Formula 1: Calculation of additional income (additional revenue – additional expenses)

$$\Delta I = (p \times fgp) - \left(cp + cp \times \frac{i}{2}\right) = p \times fgp - cp - \frac{cp}{2} \times i$$

This formula can be used to calculate the additional income at different interest rates and at different farm gate prices. To calculate the respective impact of a change in the interest rate or a change in the farm gate price on the additional in-

104 Risk mitigation through adapted loan products and lending procedures

come, one can calculate the first derivative of the equation with regard to farm gate price and the first derivative of the equation with regard to the interest rate.

First derivative with regard to farm gate price: $\Delta I'(fgp) = p = 500$	First derivative with regard to interest rate: $\Delta I'(i) = -\dfrac{cp}{2} = -\dfrac{158}{2} = -79$

The first derivative shows the change of additional income when the farm gate price or interest rate is increased by 1 unit. The values for additional productivity (p) and the additional cost of production (cp) are known and can be put into the equation. One can now see that increasing the farm gate price by 1 unit changes the additional income by 500, while increasing the interest rate by 1 unit decreases the additional income by 79. This indicates that the farm gate price has a higher influence on the income of a smallholder farmer as the interest rate.

Farm gate prices for cotton are highly volatile, as can be seen in Figure 3, which depicts the average farm gate prices paid to COMPACI cotton farmers. While farm gate prices in West Africa (Benin, Burkina Faso, Côte d'Ivoire) are announced before sowing, smallholder farmers in East Africa only learn the price they receive for their cotton at the time of selling. Smallholders in West Africa can, therefore, better plan their incomes and can calculate whether they can afford a loan, whereas farmers (and MFIs) in eastern Africa cannot make these calculations.

Figure 3: Farm gate price of seed cotton 2007–2013

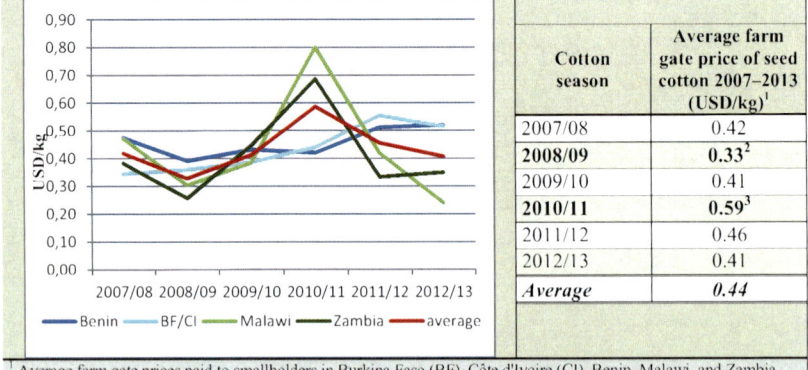

Cotton season	Average farm gate price of seed cotton 2007–2013 (USD/kg)[1]
2007/08	0.42
2008/09	0.33[2]
2009/10	0.41
2010/11	0.59[3]
2011/12	0.46
2012/13	0.41
Average	*0.44*

[1] Average farm gate prices paid to smallholders in Burkina Faso (BF), Côte d'Ivoire (CI), Benin, Malawi, and Zambia.
[2] Lowest average farm gate price in countries named above, however, lowest total farm gate price was at 0.24 USD/kg.
[3] Highest average farm gate price in countries named above, however, highest total farm gate price was at 0.80 USD/kg.
Source: own figure based on internal COMPACI project reports.

The different EIRs of the interviewed MFIs also showed a great variety ranging from 24% p.a. (Equity Bank) to 68% p.a. (CRDB) as can be seen in Table 15. CLCAMs and Equity Bank also offered to comparable loan products—one at a "subsidized" interest rate and one at an unsubsidized interest rate. "Subsidized" refers to loans that were supported through credit guarantee funds, technical assistance, and/or the involvement of other actors of the value chain for loan monitoring or loan repayment, so that the costs and risks of the respective MFI were reduced.

Table 15: Comparison of EIRs: highest vs. lowest; unsubsidized vs. subsidized

	Unsubsidized loan products—lowest vs. highest EIR		Externally subsidized vs. non-subsidized loan products of two MFIs			
			CLCAM		Equity Bank	
Type of loan	Equity Bank	CRDB	COMPACI (subsidized)	General agric. (unsubsidized)	Grain and hortic. (subsidized)	Farm input (unsubsidized)
EIR p.a.	24%	68%	19%	41%	21%	28%

Source: own figure.

Table 16 combines farm gate prices and interest rates and shows the impact of both on the additional income. Farm gate prices are not sorted by cotton season, but rather in ascending order to make it easier to read.

Table 16: Additional income at different interest rates and farm gate prices

		Unsubsidized loan products—lowest vs. highest EIR		Externally subsidized vs. non-subsidized loan products of two MFIs				
				CLCAM		Equity Bank		
		Equity Bank	CRDB	COMPACI (subsidized)	General agric. (unsubsidized)	Grain and hortic. (subsidized)	Farm input (unsubsidized)	Comparison interest rate
		24%	68%	19%	41%	21%	28%	27%
Farm gate prices	0.33	-11.96	-46.72	-8.01	-25.39	-9.59	-15.12	-14.33
	0.41	28.04	-6.72	31.99	14.61	30.41	**24.88**	25.67
	0.42	33.04	-1.72	36.99	19.61	35.41	**29.88**	**30.67**
	0.44	43.04	8.28	46.99	29.61	45.41	39.88	40.67
	0.46	53.04	18.28	56.99	39.61	55.41	49.88	50.67
	0.59	118.04	83.28	121.99	104.61	120.41	114.88	115.67

Calculated at an additional productivity of 500 kg/ha, additional input costs of 158 USD/ha and a loan term of 6 months.
Source: own table.

The red coloured fields (number in bold) show the effect on additional income of a change in interest rate by 1 percentage point (from 28% to 27%) as well as a change in farm gate price of USD 0.01 (from USD 0.42 to USD 0.41). A reduction of interest rate by 1 percentage point increases the additional income from USD 29.88 to USD 30.67, that is, by USD 0.79. An increase of farm gate prices by USD 0.01 increases the additional income by USD 5. This again illustrates the high impact of farm gate prices on the income of smallholder farmers.

Based on these findings, the strong focus of some development actors on lowering interest rates for smallholder farmers through different, often expensive, measures could be questioned. At a minimum, it is important to take a close look at the value chain and crop in question to analyse whether high interest rates or rather other factors are the main challenge. If it is the latter, as in the above example of cotton smallholder farmers where volatile market prices have a much higher impact on farmers' incomes than the level of interest rates, it would be preferable to invest the (donor) money in measures to stabilize the income of farmers via the mitigation of market price fluctuations. These measures could include better post-harvest management to ensure that the whole harvest can be sold and storage facilities, such as warehouses, combined with warehouse receipts (see Section 7.1.2). Furthermore, a price insurance product that would guarantee a minimum price would be interesting to consider. Attached to a loan product, this price insurance could mitigate the price risk for farmers as well as for MFIs, as MFIs would be insured that the smallholder can repay his/her loan through the guaranteed minimum price.

It is important to note, however, that the effect of interest rates increases with higher input costs. Moreover, should the additional productivity turn out to be lower, the effect of the farm gate prices on the farmer's income is reduced and the effect of the interest rate increases relative to the change in the farm gate price. For example, assuming that the input costs (additional costs of production) would be USD 200 instead of USD 158 and the additional productivity would be 300 kg/ha (instead of 500 kg/ha). In this scenario, a reduction of 1 percentage point in the interest rate (28–27%) would increase the income by USD 1, while a reduction in farm gate prices of USD 0.01 (from USD 0.42 to USD 0.41) would increase the income by USD 3.

7.2 Risk management through adapted lending procedures

A good **loan assessment** was seen as the key for high repayment rates at all MFIs. During the loan assessment process MFIs have to choose the "right" farmers, for example, smallholders that apply good agricultural techniques. This is especially important for agricultural lending to smallholder farmers, as specific risks in agricultural lending, such as weather and market price risks, cannot be mitigated through specific loan features or repayment incentives. Insurance products to manage these risks hardly exist in SSA. According to the Financial Development Consultant of the Agricultural Business Initiative Trust (aBi Trust) in Uganda, these external risks can be mitigated by choosing the right farmers. According to him, farmers who do timely planting apply good agricultural techniques and use improved inputs (e.g. drought-resistant seeds) can even harvest reasonable yields in unfavourable weather conditions and have high enough yields to make some profits even in case of market price drops.[112] Loan officers in agricultural lending, therefore, need profound agricultural know-how to judge whether or not farmers apply these techniques. Besides judging the capacity of smallholders, loan officers also need to assess the willingness of smallholders (i.e. "character") to repay their loans in an environment characterized by information asymmetry, which is further enhanced through long distances, poor infrastructure in rural areas, and often distorted credit cultures. As in traditional microfinance, loan officers therefore assess the five Cs, but need some specific (agricultural) knowledge to assess the different aspects, such as capacity and (market) conditions. Equity Bank's Agribusiness General Manager, therefore, stated that a sixth C has to be added in agricultural finance for smallholder farmer, namely "crops".

Table 17 compares the methods and procedures used for assessing the five Cs in traditional microfinance to the approaches applied by the interviewed MFIs for their agricultural lending to smallholder farmers. One can see from Table 17 that there are some strong similarities between traditional and agricultural microfinance approaches. Information gathering through groups, family, and friends as well as joint liability exists in both, as well the assessment of the household cash flow rather than the income from the prospective project, advising on diversified household incomes, being experienced in the business you undertake and accepting non-traditional collateral. There are, however, some important differences, which will be explained in the following paragraphs.

---

[112] This statement was also supported by the General Manager East Africa, Neumann Foundation, and the Executive Manager of the Ugandan Coffee Farmer Alliance (UCA).

108 Risk mitigation through adapted loan products and lending procedures

Table 17: Comparison of loan assessment and monitoring

Feature	Traditional microfinance	Agric. finance for smallholder farmers
Loan assessment		
Character	• Group lending • Interview family, friends, opinion leader in community • Visit household and business	• Group lending (without staggered disbursements) • Interview family, friends, local authorities, extension worker • Own contribution
Capacity to repay	• Assess business plan • Assess household (hh) cash flow *Good to have:* diversified hh income and business experience	• Assess income from agriculture • Assess hh cash flow • Interview extension worker • Assess existing value chain links (inputs, markets) *Good to have:* diversified hh income; grow different crops; have experience in commercial agriculture
Capital	(Assets and liabilities)	(Assets and liabilities)
Collateral	• Collateral substitutes: joint liability group guarantee; personal guarantors, cash collateral • Non-traditional collateral	• Collateral substitutes: joint liability (*BUT:* not against weather and market price risks!); personal guarantors; cash collateral • Non-traditional collateral
(Market) Conditions	• Business experience of borrower	• Borrower needs agricultural experience as commercial farmer • Know the crop • Know the value chain
Loan monitoring		
Repayment incentives	• Group lending: social pressure, staggered loan disbursements, group repayments • Dynamic incentives: threatening to stop lending, progressive lending • Frequent repayment installments • Public repayments	• Group repayments • Relationship to loan officer • Monitor farmer at all growing stages (planting, weeding, harvesting—especially in cases with partial loan disbursements)

Source: own table.

Group lending is also used in agricultural finance for smallholder farmers: all of the interviewed MFIs except for CRDB offered group lending, including joint group liability for agricultural clients who would not qualify for individual lending because they lack securities.[113] According to the interviews, group lending was used first and foremost to use the knowledge of group members for gaining information on the credit worthiness of different group members, secondly as social collateral, and thirdly to reduce transaction costs for training, assessing, and monitoring the farmers. Interviews conducted at Equity Bank offered the most elaborated

---

[113] It could not be assessed whether or not CRDB offers group loans at some of their other branches. At their branch in Lira, solely individual loans were offered.

insight into the MFIs' advantages of group lending. Therefore, the following mostly draws on these interviews and adds examples from other MFIs where appropriate.

At Equity Bank, the group formation process was quite important. Farmers have to form groups of 15–30 people and officially register their group. In many cases, informal farmer groups already exist, which then register and are formalized. Equity Bank also encourages smallholder group formation to buy inputs in bulk, do stocking, share agricultural practices, etc. After registration, groups are given approx. 2 months' time to meet weekly and get to know each other and the loan officer. Loan officers, also called relationship officers at Equity Bank, as it better describes their job, attend the weekly meetings and train farmers on different topics, for example, financial literacy, the importance of savings, general management of finances, record keeping and analysing whether or not an agricultural business is viable, and how to organize as a group. Smallholder farmer groups also elect officials and a credit committee. Additionally, they open a group account with which they do some weekly group savings of around the equivalent to USD 1 (USD 1 is saved per week as a group), which later serves as cash collateral. Through this process, group members get time to know each other and inform themselves about what it means to take a loan and loan officers also get to know the group.

> "We give them time (…), remember these people they need to have this cohesiveness. They have to come together and come to understand and to know each other. Because if I'm guaranteeing you, than I need to know you well. What are you doing? How are you? How is your character? So we give them time. At least it will take about 6 weeks to 2 months. (…) So that during that time and during those meetings, you go and offer them trainings, interact with them."[114]

Faulu and Juhudi Kilimo had a similarly intense process to prepare the groups before the actual loan assessment.

During loan assessment, loan officers can not only gain much information on the character, but also on the professionalism of the agricultural activity through the group members. At Equity Bank, the internal group credit committee collects the loan demands of individual group members and gives their recommendations to the loan officer. The loan officer discusses these demands with the group credit committee, but also does his/her own individual loan assessment with the applicants. Loan officers visit the individual farms, look at the farmers' fields, talk to all family members as well as local authorities and other people who know the farmers and

---

[114] Relationship Officer for Agriculture, Equity Bank, Kikuyi branch.

about their agricultural business and experiences (e.g. extension workers). During this process they very much concentrate on the overall cash flow of the household, as will be explained in further detail later. Even though it is important to do the individual assessment, the loan officer at Equity Bank's branch in Kikuyu reported that the recommendations of the group credit committee are quite reliable: "So in most of the cases, if we are advised by the group that you qualify (...), during the appraisal you find that those guys really qualify to get the funding."[115] Faulu's groups also have a credit screening team that does an initial internal loan assessment. In a second step, the group member, applying for the loan has to leave the group and the other members discuss his/her loan request, character, and agricultural experiences in the presence of a Faulu loan officer. According to Faulu, this allows the loan officer to get a thorough picture of both the character as well as the agricultural practices of a farmer (whether s/he works his/her field well or not).[116]

After loan approval, the loan is allocated to the individual account of the respective farmer and not to the group account. This was practiced by all interviewed MFIs. Agaru SACCO initially disbursed loans to a group account and the group allocated the money to the individual members. They later changed to individual disbursements after they encountered many difficulties, such as group leaders allocating less money to the individuals than was granted or running away with all of the money.[117] Generally, all group members receive their loans at the same time, because staggered disbursements, meaning that some members only receive their loan after the repayment of other group members' loans, does not work for agriculture. However, most MFIs practiced a partial disbursement of the loan based on the critical steps of the agricultural project that was undertaken to avoid loan diversion and to better monitor the smallholder farmer.

Even though the loan is disbursed to individual accounts, all interviewed MFIs channelled the *loan repayment* through the group account, for example, the whole group is responsible for repaying the cumulative loans of all group members. Since most MFIs required a monthly repayment of interest and/or small parts of the principal, the monthly amount is collected by the group officials and repaid through the group account. This reduces transaction costs for farmers, as they do not have to travel individually to the MFI to deposit their repayments. It also reduces transac-

---

[115] Relationship Officer for Agriculture, Equity Bank, Kikuyi branch.
[116] Agribusiness Development Manager, Faulu.
[117] Branch Manager, Agaru SACCO, Pader branch.

tion costs and risks for the MFI, because the group monitors and enforces the repayments of group members, but can also "jump in" if one group member is not able to meet one of the installments. During the entire process the group continues to meet on a regular basis, while the loan officer attends some of these meetings from time to time. It is thereby of special importance that loan officers know the critical steps of production and visits the farmers groups according to these stages to monitor whether borrowers are on track and prepared for the next loan disbursement. This enables loan officers to find out about any occurring difficulties (e.g. death of some financed animals or crop diseases) and to discuss the issue with the borrower. They can also adapt the following loan disbursement accordingly or even stop it, which reduces the amount of the loan that can fall into default. Additionally, many MFIs reported that they supported farmers with agricultural advice during the agricultural season and/or were able to link farmer groups to extension agents, development organizations, or the MoA in case of difficulties affecting several farmers (e.g. crop disease).[118]

In summary, group lending in agriculture reduces transaction costs, as many farmers can be reached at the same time and information gathering for loan assessment is partly outsourced to the group. Similarly, group liability motivates smallholder farmers to monitor and support each other in the utilization of good agricultural practices and other behaviour to ensure individual repayment. However, group lending cannot mitigate covariant risks such as weather extremes that cause (crop) failure for all farmers in a respective area. Additionally, regular group repayments do not necessarily imply that the agricultural activities are on track (as is the case in traditional microfinance), since the monthly repayments can also come from other household sources and thus loan officers still have to be in the field monitoring and keeping in touch with the smallholder farmers.

All MFIs except for CLCAMs and MC²s *analysed the whole household cash flow* during the loan assessment to appraise the repayment capacity and decide on the repayment schedule. They do so because they realized that most farmers have diversified household incomes from various agricultural as well as non-agricultural sources, enabling them to meet their daily needs until harvest time of

---

[118] Agribusiness Development Manager, Faulu; Executive Secretary, ADAF; Accountant, ADAF; Manager Loans and Agricultural System Administrator, Agaru SACCO; Consultant for Performance Management, Juhudi Kilimo; Relationship Officer for Agriculture, Equity Bank, Kikuyu branch.

the main crops they wish to fund (e.g. they have different crops, some animals, small grocery shop, etc.). Such a diversified household income was actually welcomed and often requested by all of the interviewed MFIs. First, it reduces the vulnerability of the farming household to external shocks and thus also the risk for the MFI. Even in case of weather extremes, farmers have alternative sources of income they can use for living expenses and repaying the loan. Secondly, a steady and regular source of off-farm income sustaining the household until harvest and enabling them meeting their daily needs, reduces the risk that the loan will be consumed for family needs instead of using it for the agricultural activity.[119] CRDB even has a requirement for farmers to have small off-farm side incomes and to grow at least two or three different crops, so that if one fails they can repay the loan through the other activities.[120] Christen/Pearce (2005, 14) also found that

> "A number of microfinance institutions that have developed stable agricultural lending portfolios also minimize risk by excluding households that rely on only one or perhaps two crops and have no off-farm income."

Repayments are then structured according to the household cash flow, mostly allowing for unequal installments, grace periods, regular interest payments only or any other type of irregular payment plan. The interviewed MFIs mentioned several advantages of assessing the whole cash flow and combining it with regular (interest) repayments. First, taking a (micro-) loan has an impact on the whole family. Assessing the whole cash flow and thereby also interviewing family members, therefore, assures that all of them agree on the loan and understand that it has to be repaid independently of the actual loan purpose and success or failure of the funded project. Secondly, the MFI may see other activities it could fund besides or in addition to the agricultural project. Thirdly, smallholder farmers are regularly reminded of their loan through small regular repayments. Fourthly, regular repayments reduce the burden of external circumstances that lead to a failure of the project (e.g. weather extremes—if half of the loan is already repaid the burden is no longer that high).

During loan assessment, loan officers also find out whether a farmer is a **commercial farmer with adequate agricultural experience,** generally meaning at least one crop cycle for the plant s/he wishes to fund. This was an eligibility criteri-

---

[119] Agribusiness General Manager, Equity Bank.
[120] Loan Officer for Agriculture, CRDB, Lira branch.

on at all MFIs. Commercial farmer thereby means that farmers have a business mind-set and want to produce for the market and not just for subsistence—it does not mean that s/he must farm on a large scale. The Relationship Officer for Agriculture at Equity Bank's Kikuyu branch described his expectations on farmers as follows:

> "I expect you have established relations, in terms of where do I buy my agrochemicals, where do I buy my seeds, who visits my farm in case of extension services and where do I sell my tomatoes. So that at least I require you to have experience. I don't give you money, go and start up a business, then 3,4,5,6 months, you think 'Oh this is not the kind of business I would have wanted to do.' But you already invested money. (...) So that's why we want at least when we're funding, that at least you have done a cycle or a crop."[121]

And CRDB reported that

> "The Bank is very careful in selecting commercially-oriented farmers, irrespective of the size of their operation. The farmer must have experience of at least one season, with evidence of surplus incomes from agricultural production and other sources. The farmers must target a specific market, either through collective marketing with other farmers, by doing contract farming or by selling to nearby markets or traders." (Kyanika Nsibambi 2010, 45)

To assess the experience of the farmer as well as the cash flow of a farming household, loan officers need to have a thorough understanding of agriculture and need to be in the field with farmers. According to the Relationship Officer for Agriculture at Equity Bank's Kikuyu branch, agricultural loan officers spend 80% of their time outside the branch:

> "We don't make our decisions based on the account, because if you look at the nature of agriculture, the farms maybe are very far away from the bank. So those guys may not really do a lot of banking. But when you go to the field you are able at least to see what they have been doing. It even becomes easier to make a decision from the field. So our main appraisal and decision making is based on what we have in the field."[122]

Since farmers not only do not do much banking, but also do not have established record keeping about their agricultural activities or their household incomes and expenses, loan officers need to ask a lot of questions during their first loan assessment interview. Some of the topics they try to investigate are the kind of crops a farmer cultivates, how many bags s/he has sold, how often s/he sold them, how

---

[121] Relationship Officer for Agriculture, Equity Bank, Kikuyu branch.
[122] Relationship Officer for Agriculture, Equity Bank, Kikuyu branch.

much s/he is making, what the spouse or other family members are doing, how much they earn, how many children they have, whether they go to school, how much money they spend on school fees and on water and electricity bills, etc. Here, the agricultural background of loan officers is again required to evaluate whether or not the farmers' information is correct and implies that the smallholder practices good agricultural techniques. The loan officer needs to be able to know whether answers to questions like how many bags of fertilizer the smallholder farmer used for one hectare of maize, how much s/he produced on his/her field or which steps s/he follows and where s/he needs financing correspond to the recommendations for the specific crop in this specific area or not. They also need to know the average prices for the different inputs as well as the average market prices to assess the actual cash flow and repayment capacity. For the first loan assessment, Equity Bank produces this balance sheet together with the farmer, but recommends her/him to do it independently for the following years and requires it for a second loan.[123] MC²s and CLCAMs reported that they developed a detailed commodity profile with all relevant information on production costs and possible returns for different agricultural products for their loan officers to see whether the information a farmer is giving makes sense or seem to be unrealistic.[124] Literature suggests that some MFIs also developed credit scoring for their smallholder lending, but none of the interviewed MFI did so.[125]

Equity Bank's Agribusiness General Manager stated that the whole process of group building, training groups, attending regular group meetings, doing a thorough household cash flow assessment as well as intense monitoring is much cost intensive, meaning the first loan for a new customer/smallholder can hardly be profitable for the MFI. Any following loan is, however, much cheaper and the bank starts to earn money with its lending activities. Equity Bank's goal is, therefore, to get long-term customers among smallholder farmers and their whole customer relationship agenda builds on this, for example, focusing on the relationship between loan officer and borrowers and calling loan officers relationship officers; trying to

---

[123] Credit Officer for Agriculture, Equity Bank, Kikuyu branch.
[124] Head of Accounting and Control of MicroBank Department, ADAF; General Manager, CLCAM. Pehunco; General Manager, CLCAM Kouandé.
[125] More information on credit scoring for agricultural lending in development countries can be found in the webinar of AgriFin (2013), where, that is, the Frankfurt School of Finance explains its Agricultural Loan Evaluation System.

meet all financial needs of smallholders (including social needs at loan terms suiting agricultural activities), etc.

Many of the interviewed MFIs also stated that they did have some difficulties due to distorted credit cultures among smallholder farmers, when they first started agricultural finance for smallholders. Smallholders often perceive loans as government handouts. This notion became even more as soon as farmers found out that some development agency or government programme was supporting the respective MFI in their lending activities, for example, through guarantee funds or others (farmers were often aware of this as government, in particular, tried to catch votes by announcing that they support agricultural lending in radio shows, etc.). In their first years, many MFIs, therefore, had to embark on tough recovery processes to break this notion of loans being handouts. Even when the recovery processes was more costly than the actual outstanding loans, however, MFIs reported that it was worth embarking on these tough processes as they helped to change smallholders' perception of credits and were a statement to both current and future clients that the MFI is serious about repayment.[126]

---

[126] Agribusiness General Manager, Equity Bank; Agribusiness Development Manager, Faulu; Manager Loans and Agricultural System Administrator, Agaru SACCO; Kyanika Nsimbambi 2010, 42.

8 Further strategies to reduce risks and transaction costs in agricultural lending to smallholder farmers

Adapting loan features and lending procedures helped MFI mitigating risks and costs in agricultural finance for smallholder farmers. There are, however, some overarching features that were named in all of the interviews. Since most of them have already been mentioned in previous chapters, this chapter will only provide a summary of the key messages.

8.1 Qualified staff with agricultural backgrounds

The importance of qualified staff with agricultural backgrounds for loan development, loan assessment, and the monitoring of agricultural loans for smallholder farmers has already been emphasized in the previous chapters. Most of the interviewed MFIs even rated it as *the* most important element for successful agricultural microfinance. Christen/Pearce (2005, 24) also emphasized that "the few microfinance programmes that have expanded into agricultural activities have found it desirable to hire agronomists and veterinarians to support loan decisions and methodologies". The following section will, therefore, summarize the key messages on qualified staff in agricultural lending to smallholder farmers.

According to the interviewed MFIs, staff with agricultural backgrounds is needed at different levels: at the headquarters to develop new agricultural loan products and at the branches to work as loan officers. Loan officers with an agricultural background are able to analyse agricultural projects and to identify whether the information on field size, required inputs and anticipated outputs are realistic. Smallholder farmers often over or underestimate their acreage, which leads to a miscalculation of their cash flows regarding their agricultural business.[127] Loan officers need to be able to tell whether a crop or an animal is well cared for during loan monitoring and for determining partial loan disbursements:

> "(…) when I come to your farm, just from the look I can tell what the acreage is. If I come for a post disbursement to visit, I will tell whether this crop is not doing well or is doing

---

[127] Agribusiness General Manager, Equity Bank. A study conducted for COMPACI in Malawi also showed that smallholders over or underestimated their cotton field size by around 50% when compare to GPS measurement.

118 Further strategies to reduce risks and transaction costs in agricultural lending

> well or you have not applied fertilizer, you have not added top dressing, you did not do the right thing. (...) you can only follow it up with somebody who really understands."[128]

Staff with agricultural backgrounds is also needed to keep up to date with agriculturally relevant data, such as market and input prices as well as meteorological data, and they need to be able to draw the right conclusions from it. CRDB reported that their close contact with the meteorological department, which provides weather information and forecasts for their different areas of operation, helped them a lot in 2011:

> "This year, there was for example a drought threat and this [information from the metrological department, the author] helped the bank a lot, because the bank was able to advise the farmers to delay the planting a bit and wait for the rains. And also they were able to structure their payments considering that there will be a drought at the end of the year, so they were giving them more grace period to cover for the months were there was drought."[129]

Furthermore, Equity Bank stated that loan officers with agricultural backgrounds have a different attitude towards working with smallholder farmers and are willing to leave their office to meet smallholders in the field. This helps them to build up the necessary relationship of mutual trust, as smallholders often shy away from banks. Loan officers who attend farmers' meetings, visit smallholders at their farms, know about the way of life in villages and are able to give advice on different crops and good agricultural practices and are able to build trust and familiarize smallholders with MFIs. At Equity, the close relationship between loan officer and customer is part of their corporate identity and thought to be a key element of economic success—also in terms of repayment rates, since their experience shows that borrowers are keen to repay a friend (e.g. also a loan officer perceived as friend) but not necessarily a bank. To underline their role, loan officers at Equity Bank are called relationship officers.[130]

Most of the interviewed MFIs strongly connected the performance of their agricultural portfolio to the agricultural background of their loan officers. Equity Bank, CRDB, and Agaru SACCO stated that their agricultural lending business suf-

---

[128] Agribusiness General Manager, Equity Bank.
[129] Loan Officer for Agriculture, CRDB, Lira branch.
[130] Agribusiness General Manager, Equity Bank.

fered from some weaknesses until they started to recruit agronomists.[131] As can be seen in Table 18, most MFIs employed or were planning to employ loan officers with an agricultural background at the time of the interview. While Equity Bank had already recruited 200 agronomists and CRDB 100, Agaru SACCO had hired several agricultural extension workers to work as loan officers. Equity Bank thereby strongly opted to employ agronomists rather than training existing loan officers in agriculture as the Agribusiness General Manager at Equity Bank stated that "you can't turn a banker into an agronomist, but an agronomist into a banker". This is, however, quite costly, which was also the reason why not all MFIs had been able to hire agronomists, especially at the beginning of their agricultural operations. Faulu, therefore, chose to offer agricultural training to their existing loan officers.

Table 18: Educational background of agricultural loan officers

	CB			MFC		MBFI		
	Equity	CRDB	Faulu	Juhudi Kilimo	RUCREF	Agaru SACCO	CLCAM	MC²
Loan officers' background	Agric.	Agric.	Finance with training in agric.	Agric.	Finance; want to recruit agric.	Agric.	Finance	Finance, want to recruit agric.

Agric. = agricultural background, mostly agronomists.
Source: own table based on interviews with MFIs.

8.2 Value chain finance

"You cannot do agricultural lending in isolation; you cannot just isolate and fund the farmer without thinking about the market, without thinking about the transport. So you just not work in isolation. That is what I realized. You need the other actors in the value chain for you to be effective."[132]

Faulu's Agribusiness Development Manager offered the above statement when asked about the most important lesson he learned about agricultural finance at Faulu. Financial institutions traditionally focus on the direct recipient of a loan and his/her economic activities and securities. Looking at the whole agricultural value chain and understanding the risks and opportunities of the sector as a whole allows for products that best fit the needs of the respective actors in the chain to be designed and to reduce the transaction costs and risks of lending. All of the inter-

---

[131] Agribusiness General Manager, Equity Bank; Loan Officer for Agriculture, CRDB, Lira branch; Manager Loans and Agricultural System Administrator, Agaru SACCO.
[132] Agribusiness Development Manager, Faulu.

120 Further strategies to reduce risks and transaction costs in agricultural lending

viewed MFIs claimed to have a value chain approach in their agricultural lending. Their understanding of value chain finance was, however, varied.

Miller/Jones' (2010, 2)[133] definition of value chain finance will be used to approach the existing different perceptions of value chain finance. They define value chain finance as "the flows of fund to and among the various links within a value chain" and distinguish between internal and external value chain finance as follows:

> "Internal Value chain finance is that which takes place within the value chain such as when an input supplier provides credit to a farmer, or when a lead firm advances funds to a market intermediary.
> External value chain finance is that which is made possible by value chain relationships and mechanisms: for example, a bank issues a loan to farmers based on a contract with a trusted buyer or a warehouse receipt from a recognized storage facility." (Miller/ Jones 2010, 2)

Value chain finance provided by MFIs is, based on this definition, always external value chain finance. Agricultural finance for smallholder farmers can thus only be defined as external value chain finance if there is a direct correlation to the value chain, for example, based on a contractual relationship. While some of the interviewed MFIs offered external value chain finance in the defined sense by collaborating with other actors of the chain through contractual relationships, others "just" offered loans to smallholder farmers and tried to *understand* the whole value chain in which "their" smallholder is involved in. Even though this would not qualify as external value chain finance under the above definition, it is important to be able to anticipate the existing costs and risks of the value chain.

The following experiences regarding value chain finance were mentioned during the interviews. The first two rather fall under the category "understanding value chains" while the latter are examples of value chain finance as defined by Miller/Jones (2010, 2).

First, Equity, CRDB, and Juhudi Kilimo offered financial products for all actors along a value chain to make sure that financial constraints do not hinder the chain from functioning well.[134] According to the Agribusiness General Manager of Equity Bank, it is important to address all financial needs of a value chain, even if

---
[133] Miller/Jones (2010) book "Agricultural value chain finance. Tools and Lessons" is the most comprehensive book in the field of value chain finance and can highly be recommended.
[134] Agribusiness General Manager, Equity Bank; Consultant for Performance Management, Juhudi Kilimo; Kyanika Nsibambi 2010, 44.

the main focus is on financing smallholder producers, because "a [value] chain is as strong as its weakest link". Offering loans for smallholder farmers, therefore, makes only sense if the other actors in the chain do not face financial constraints themselves and can meet increased demands, for example, for improved inputs:

> "So much as our focus is here, on production, we realize, if we empower the farmer here, but the stockiest who is supposed to provide good seed and fertilizer is not at the level of the farmer, it does not work. What happens: we have a demand here that this person cannot meet. Yet we want to be sure that if we grant you a loan, you're able to buy good seed, certified seed, you're able to buy good fertilizer. So by the virtue of financing farmers for production, we find ourselves very much also financing stockiest."[135]

Secondly, understanding the entire value chain is important to tailor the financial products to the respective needs of chain participants and to properly assess risks during loan assessment. Juhudi Kilimo felt that their thorough knowledge of the dairy value chain and the long process of developing and fine-tuning their loan products, lending mechanisms, and support services for different actors all along the chain was the key to their high repayment rates.[136] Faulu and RUCREF, on the other hand, stated that their lack of value chain analysis lead to their initial failure in lending to smallholder farmers. After addressing this problem and conducting a proper value chain analysis, Faulu changed their loan products for cereal farmers by introducing a compulsory cereal insurance product and identifying qualified input suppliers to cooperate with. Additionally, they improved their overall knowledge on cereal farming and thus their loan assessment.[137] RUCREF, on the other hand, used a value chain analysis to assess the financial needs and risks of different value chains and at different levels of these value chains. They found some financial constraints higher up the value chain, where risks for MFIs were also lower, thus offering them a good entry point into agricultural finance.[138]

Thirdly, some of the interviewed MFIs were also involved in external value chain finance as defined above. They cooperated with other value chain participants to reduce their lending risks and costs. CRDB has a strong focus on contract farmers, as the farmers' lack of market access had caused many defaults in the past (Kyanika Nsibambi 2010, 47ff.). Equity Bank, which started its agricultural lending

---

[135] Agribusiness General Manager, Equity Bank.
[136] Consultant for Performance Management, Juhudi Kilimo.
[137] Agribusiness Development Manager, Faulu.
[138] Agricultural Product Specialist, RUCREF.

122 Further strategies to reduce risks and transaction costs in agricultural lending

with contracted tea farmers, also stated that working with contract farmers is one of the easier ways to finance agriculture, as farmers have assured markets and sometimes also receive their inputs from the lead firm.[139] Equity Bank also addresses the issue of loan diversion through cooperation with input dealers in some regions. Instead of providing cash loans, smallholder farmers receive vouchers for inputs, which they can redeem at the input dealers' shops. Input providers are directly paid by the bank.[140] And Faulu was able to reduce their interest rates for dairy loans through a collaboration with dairy co-operatives that directly deducts the loan repayment before paying the smallholder farmer. This greatly reduces transaction costs and risks for Faulu.[141]

The COMPACI loan for smallholder cotton farmers provided by CLCAMs in Benin is an example of a complex cooperation between different actors of the value chain that shows both the potential and the difficulties of external value chain finance. COMPACI is active in the northern part of Benin, where cotton producers have difficulties in accessing credits. CLCAMs were reluctant to lend to cotton producers and others due to smallholders' high indebtedness following the cotton crisis, but also due to a lack of adapted loan products (no long-term loan for agricultural equipment, high interest rates). In 2009, COMPACI funded a study to develop a credit mechanism that reduces MFIs' risks through collaboration with different stakeholders in the cotton value chain and allows the MFI to offer loans for draft animals, equipment, and cotton harvest at lower interest rates (12% instead of 24% p.a.). The value chain credit scheme included eight different stakeholders: CeCPA/CeRPA (Centre Communale/Regionale pour la Promotion d'Agriculture), AIC, the cotton producer co-operatives, CSPR (Centrale de Sécurisation de Paiement et de Recouvrement) COBEMAG, MFIs, COMPACI programme and the cotton ginneries (Figure 4). In 2010, CLCAMs started issuing loans under this scheme.

---

[139] Agribusiness General Manager, Equity Bank.
[140] Agribusiness General Manager, Equity Bank.
[141] Agribusiness Development Manager, Faulu.

Figure 4: External value chain finance for cotton smallholders in Benin

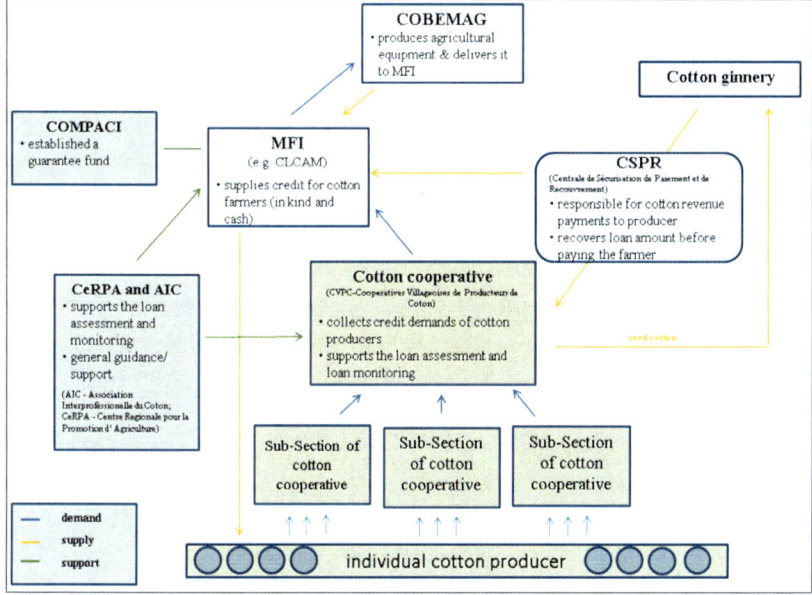

Source: own figure.

Figure 4 illustrates the mechanism of the credit scheme: the individual cotton farmers channel their credit demand to the CLCAM through their cotton co-operative. Extension officers from CeRPA, who know the cotton farmers through their regular training sessions, support the loan assessment. They discuss the loan applications of individual cotton farmers with the group leaders of the cotton co-operative and both agree on the loan applications before forwarding it to the CLCAM. The CLCAMs review and verify the loan applications, discuss it with the group leaders of the cotton co-operative and the extension agents and perform cross-checks through field visits. They do not, however, visit every applicant, thus relying on the recommendations of the co-operative and the extension agents:

> "On selectionne les dossiers, on ne peut pas toutpart courir. La ou il y a plus de milles dossiers, si on veut toutpart courir ca Durant toute l'annee. Donc on peut choisir une certaine, (…) on va voir."[142]

---

[142] General Manager, CLCAM Kouandé.

This significantly reduces the costs of loan assessments. After the loan is approved, cotton farmers receive their loans individually. Agricultural equipment bought on credit is thereby directly delivered by COBEMAG (a firm that produces agricultural equipment) to the MFI and forwarded on to the smallholder, that is, the smallholder farmer receives his/her agricultural equipment in kind.

The repayment is structured as follows: cotton farmers deliver their seed cotton to the cotton ginnery. The payment to the farmer is channelled through CSPR (a sub-organization of AIC). CSPR recovers the loan amount and repays the credit before paying the farmer. Additionally, COMPACI established a loan guarantee fund of 100,000 EUR at CLCAMs piloting the credit scheme to further reduce the risk.[143] The benefits of this approach are obvious: MFIs reduce their lending risks and transaction costs, as they receive loan assessment and monitoring support by CeRPA and AIC and their loan repayments are secured through the direct loan deduction by CSPR. This allowed CLCAMs to lower their quoted interest rates by 12% p.a. (from 24% to 12% p.a.).

One major difficulty was, however, encountered during the process. AIC, being an association representing cotton ginners and farmers, is closely associated with the government (the cotton sector in Benin is only partly privatized and heavily influenced by government interference) and did not sign the mutual agreement. Their rejection to sign the contract was, however, not openly announced. The signing was postponed several times and only totally rejected in 2012. Some CLCAMs had, therefore, already started offering loans at interest rates of 12 p.a. in 2010, assuming that AIC would sign the contract and meet their obligations of deducting loan repayments before paying farmers. This was not the case and CLCAMs had to recuperate the loans themselves, which posed great difficulties to them. They had to visit farmers on their farms, in the market places and wherever else they could find them to collect the repayments. There were high default rates and they were unable to cover their costs with the low interest rate they offered.[144] Consequently, they did not offer new loans under this scheme in 2011 and when AIC finally announced their non-participation in the agreement in 2012, the value chain scheme was put on hold. As the whole cotton sector in Benin is currently "again in turmoil" (ICAC 2013, 4) and AIC was replaced by an interim committee steering the cotton sector,

---

[143] General Manager, CLCAM Pehunco; Consultant for Microfinance and value chain finance, COMPACI Benin.
[144] General Manager, CLCAM Pehunco.

the value chain approach described above might be revived with different stakeholders once the reorganization of the sector is completed.

There are, nevertheless, two interesting observations from the first attempt to set up this value chain scheme. First, the whole mechanism could not have been set up without the external assistance of COMPACI, which paid for a feasibility study and a local consultant to design the mechanism and to get all of the partners to agree to participate. In general, it may be difficult for any single participant of a value chain to initiate such a value chain financing approach, as the initial costs for the design and set-up can be quiet high and time consuming. Secondly, it can be difficult to secure the participation and committed cooperation of all necessary stakeholders. Mutual trust as well as ownership of the mechanism by all stakeholders is important. Even though a thorough assessment could not be made, not all stakeholders seemed to gain from the loan scheme, which might have been the reason why AIC decided not to participate.[145]

8.3 Cooperation with external actors

All of the interviewed MFIs collaborated with several external actors, for example, NGOs, development agencies, governments, extension services, etc. According to the Agricultural Product Specialist at RUCREF "There is nowhere a MFI will work with a farmer and will be able to work profitable by himself. The partnerships must be there. They must be there." Two different forms of partnerships can be distinguished; first, cooperation with external actors that support the MFI's lending activities, for example, through technical support or guarantee funds; and secondly cooperation with organizations that support smallholder farmers, for example, by offering them extension services, support in group formation, market linkages, or market information. These organizations not only have a good understanding of the agricultural expertise and character of "their" farmers that can be used during loan assessment, but also support farmers in being more profitable and thus more bankable.

Many smallholder farmers are (financially) illiterate, do not practice record-keeping and, therefore, do not know whether they actually make a profit or not, as all household incomes are intertwined. Financing such a smallholder is either not possible for an MFI or very costly, as the MFI has to train and prepare the farmers

---

[145] It is assumed that AIC feared to lose reputation among farmers when they deduct the loan repayment and thus paid less money to the farmers.

as well as engage in costly loan assessments. Most of the interviewed MFIs offer such training and preparation for smallholder farmers. It makes it much easier for an MFI, however, if an external organization is in charge of some of the capacity building. The Agribusiness General Manager of Equity Bank expresses it in the following way:

> "We are working a lot with partners. (...) They really help us in getting clients. (...) when other partners come in, they are able to do what the bank can't do. (...) there is so much capacity that has to be built so that farmers reach the point of funding. You see now that makes the work of the bank really easy as opposed to when we approach the farmers ourselves, we take them through training, now we start lending. When somebody is able to help us with the training and the capacity building of the farmers and we are left to, just to administer the loans and monitoring, it's easier. Sometimes they help us in monitoring and evaluation, which is also easier for the bank, because all this involves the bank's money."

Besides working with these partners, Equity Bank also closely collaborates with the local offices of the MoA to receive updated information on relevant agricultural events.[146]

Many of the interviewed MFIs also received support from donors or governments to help develop their agricultural loan products, train their agricultural loan officers, or roll out their lending activities to other branches, etc.[147] While all of the MFIs strongly appreciated this support, some also raised some of the following concerns.[148] First, most support, especially if it concerns larger amounts of money, is subject to certain conditions, for example, lower interest rates for smallholder farmers or outreach in specific, less-favoured regions. MFIs need to calculate whether these conditions are feasible as a "business option" or not, as they want to continue offering loans to their clients even after the funding stops. If they offered specific low-interest rates with which they cannot cover their operational costs, they would have to stop offering this product as soon as the funding stops. Secondly, if donors or governments openly advertise their support for specific MFIs and/or loan products, repayment rates can drop, as clients then perceive the loans as handouts. Thirdly, the support for agricultural finance for smallholder farmers in

---

[146] Agribusiness General Manager, Equity Bank.
[147] Manager Loans and Agricultural System Administrator, Agaru SACCO; Consultant for Performance Management, Juhudi Kilimo; Agribusiness General Manager, Equity Bank; Kyanika Nsibambi 2010, 44.
[148] Agribusiness General Manager, Equity Bank; Agribusiness Development Manager, Faulu; Financial Development Consultant, aBi Trust; Consultant for Microfinance and Value Chain Finance, COMPACI Benin.

SSA has been in vogue over the last few years. There is the danger that MFIs getting involved in agricultural finance for smallholders could skim off some of these funds without having a strong internal motivation to go into this kind of business. The previous chapters showed that agricultural lending for smallholder farmers involves many changes to traditional microfinance and all of the interviewed MFIs had an inherent motivation and drive to serve smallholders. It is questionable whether they would have been successful without having smallholder finance as part of their corporate mission. Getting into agricultural finance for smallholder farmers to skim off donor funds is, therefore, prone to fail.

8.4 Cost-effective outreach to smallholder farmers

The previous chapter showed that agricultural lending for smallholder farmers implies high transaction costs for both MFIs and smallholder farmers. Loan officers spend several hours per day on their motorcycles or on public transport to visit their clients in remote rural areas for loan assessment and monitoring. Smallholder, on the other hand, have to travel to the MFI to access their accounts and repay the money, as loan officers were not allowed to handle cash. To minimize these costs, all MFIs tried to interact with smallholder farmers through groups. This can, but does not necessarily have to be, combined with group lending. Simply meeting several individual farmers at once for loan assessment, monitoring, providing general advice, etc. reduces outreach costs. If group lending is added, repayments can be collected through a group account, which allows the group to handle overdue repayments of individual group members themselves and loan repayments can be made through the group account. This means only one farmer has to travel to the bank to deposit the money.[149] Some MFIs also operate satellite offices or mini branches in remote areas that are only operational several days per month (e.g. during market days), to offer further banking services to their customers (cash withdrawal, savings, etc.).[150]

Lending to farmer co-operatives that on-lend the money to their members at their own risk is another alternative to reduce costs, as the MFI only has to deal

---

[149] General Manager, CLCAM Pehunco; Manager Loans and Agricultural System Administrator, Agaru SACCO; Consultant for Performance Management, Juhudi Kilimo.
[150] General Manager, CLCAM Pehunco; Agribusiness General Manager, Equity Bank; Agribusiness Development Manager, Faulu; Consultant for Performance Management, Juhudi Kilimo; Loan Officer for Agriculture, CRDB, Lira branch.

with one customer, that is, the co-operative. It is, however, not always easy to find well-managed farmer co-operatives.[151] CBs can also partner with local MFIs to extend their outreach into rural areas. The partnership between MC²s and Afriland First Bank is such an example. The MC² can offer (international) money transfer services to their members and have access to credit lines through their partnership with Afriland First Bank, while Afriland First Bank can access rural savings, for example, by offering MC²s save deposit accounts for their excess liquidity at their bank.

Reaching smallholder farmers and rural customers through technical innovations[152]

Technical innovations such as mobile money and cell phone banking can also effectively increase the outreach of MFIs at reduced costs. The following examples mostly draw on the experience of Equity Bank, as it was the most advanced in this field.

Mobile Bank Branch Offices—Equity Bank had already started developing innovative mechanisms for reaching the rural population in the 1990s after their reorganization as a bank and reorientation on the provision of microfinance services. Their next goal was to increase the customer basis in rural areas. Since the establishment of permanent stationary branch offices in remote areas was not economically feasible, Equity Bank began deploying two four-wheel Land Cruisers as mobile bank offices. Once the profitability of these mobile offices became clear, Equity Bank successfully applied for a loan of USD 411,000 from DFID (UK) to integrate modern technology into their Land Cruisers and to increase their portfolio of mobile financial services. Today, Equity Bank can offer nearly every financial service in remote areas through their 54 mobile offices thanks to satellite-supported communication systems that allow for constant contact with the next-closest stationary branch office and a connection to Equity Bank's central database (Pearce/Reinsch 2006, 46ff.). Once a week the mobile offices drive to the various locations at set times to offer financial services for a small fee. Since they primarily operate in areas with a high population density (more than 300 persons per km²), they often service up to 3,000 customers with each mobile office and are easily able to cover their operating costs (Johnson et al. 2005, 13; Kibaara 2006, 17).

---

[151] Executive Secretary of ADAF, ADAF; Agribusiness General Manager, Equity Bank; Kyanika Nsibambi 2010, 47.
[152] The following subsection draws on Röttger (2012).

Mobile phone banking – In March of 2007, Safaricom, a member of the Vodafon Group, began offering branchless banking services for people without bank accounts through M-Pesa. M-Pesa allows money to be transferred between two people with a mobile telephone as well as for invoices and wages to be paid via mobile phone or money to be put into savings in a virtual M-Pesa account. M-Pesa agents serve as an interface between the customer and the virtual mobile money. Customers can either deposit their money into a virtual account and/or have it paid out by one of the many M-Pesa agents. As of September 2013, there were approx. 40,000 M-Pesa agents in the country and M-Pesa was used by more than 15 million people in Kenya (Safaricom 2013).

Equity Bank quickly recognized M-Pesa's potential and began cooperating with Safaricom to link a banking account to the M-Pesa system. This account was called M-Kesho and was initiated in May 2010. Figure 5 shows the mechanism and cash flows of M-Kesho.

Figure 5: M-Kesho money flow and charges

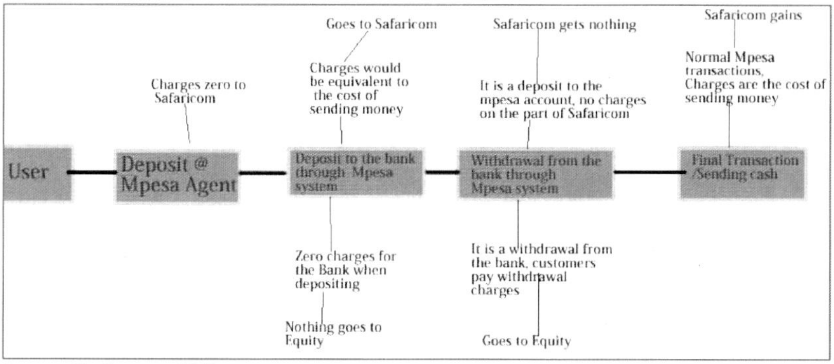

[Figure: Flow diagram showing User → Deposit @ Mpesa Agent → Deposit to the bank through Mpesa system → Withdrawal from the bank through Mpesa system → Final Transaction/Sending cash. Annotations above: "Goes to Safaricom / Charges zero to Safaricom"; "Charges would be equivalent to the cost of sending money"; "Safaricom gets nothing / It is a deposit to the mpesa account, no charges on the part of Safaricom"; "Safaricom gains / Normal Mpesa transactions, Charges are the cost of sending money". Annotations below: "Zero charges for the Bank when depositing / Nothing goes to Equity"; "It is a withdrawal from the bank, customers pay withdrawal charges / Goes to Equity".]

Source: Kachwanya 2010.

M-Pesa customers can open this bank account, which allows them to transfer money from their virtual M-Pesa account to the free M-Kesho account with Equity. The M-Kesho account pays interest on accounts with a balance starting at 1 ksh (USD 0.01). Customers can also use M-Kesho accounts to apply for short-term emergency micro-credit lines between 100 Ksh and 5,000 Ksh (USD 1–USD 56) and can take out accident micro-insurance policies. This account grants simple access to savings options and bank services to many people who did not have a bank account and allows Equity Bank to cost-effectively increase its customer base. Customers can also use M-Pesa and/or M-Kesho to pay back loans, which saves what is often a long trip to a bank office in rural areas (Safaricom 2013; Equity Bank 2013c).[153] Additionally, all common bank accounts at Equity Bank can be managed via mobile phone just like standard online banking. Customers can transfer money to other bank accounts as well as M-Pesa or orange money clients, pay bills, get bank statements, repay loans, and access small emergency loans (Equity Bank 2013c).

Agency banking—Agency banking was introduced by Equity Bank in 2010 and is primarily intended to quickly and affordably expand the bank's reach at the village level. Agents are respected persons in their communities and are long-standing customers at Equity. They own a small business with which they regularly generate turnover to ensure that they always have a sufficient supply of cash to meet the withdrawal needs of the bank's customers. In areas that Equity Bank cannot reach due to poor infrastructure, security issues or other requirements of the Central Bank that Equity Bank cannot meet in these areas, agents are the representatives of the bank and can execute bank transactions. These transactions include savings deposits, cash withdrawals, and loan repayments as well as receiving loan applications and applications to open a bank account. Agents use their own money for these transactions and offer these banking services as an additional business with which they earn money through commissions per transaction. Although agency banking was primarily developed for rural areas according to Equity's 2010 financial report, a large number of these Equity Bank agents can also be found in Kenya's cities (Equity Bank 2011, 14).[154]

---

[153] Agribusiness General Manager, Equity Bank.
[154] Agribusiness General Manager, Equity Bank.

9 Conclusion

Even though traditional microfinance has successfully paved the way for offering financial services to low-income populations, smallholder farmers in rural areas have been largely excluded. While MFIs have demonstrated that serving low-income clients can be profitable and low-income loan recipients can be creditworthy, applying proven microfinance lending techniques directly to smallholder farmers has proved to be difficult. For example, smallholder farmers cannot service quick and frequent repayments, be part of groups for which only staggered loan disbursements are offered or meet the criteria that the use of proceeds does not finance the central source of household income. Lending to smallholder farmers requires MFIs to move away from or adapt the very criteria that have proved successful in mitigating credit risk to low-income populations and as such carries with it the perception of higher risks. In addition, serving smallholder farmers exposes MFIs to further risks and costs inherent in agricultural finance (external risks, market price risk, high transaction costs associated with serving remote areas).

The MFIs interviewed for the purpose of this paper showed, however, that a combination of well-working traditional microfinance mechanisms together with an adaptation of the above-mentioned features to agriculture can work for smallholder farmers and MFIs. Although the MFIs interviewed come from various institutional backgrounds (CBs, microfinance companies, membership-based institutions) with different motivations and strategies for entering the agricultural microfinance sector, their strategies for adapting loan features and lending techniques for smallholder farmers showed a number of similarities.

The most common adaptations in terms of loan features relate to loan term and payment schedule. Loan terms were increased to be long enough to cover one agricultural (crop) cycle and flexible repayment schedules were introduced, allowing for grace periods and lump sum repayments uncommon in traditional microfinance loans; both changes leading to increased MFI risk. One way MFIs mitigate associated risks is by taking advantage of farmers' non-harvest-related income streams to introduce regular interest payments or, if possible, regular small principal repayments (depending on the total household cash flow), which serve as regular reminders to farmers of their outstanding debt. Another common adaptation relates to joint group liability as a collateral substitute. Unlike traditional microfinance, it is not possible to enforce group pressure by staggering loan disbursements within the smallholder farmers' group, as in this case all members must receive their loans at the same time, to meet the needs of the cultivation cycle. To mitigate this risk, MFIs introduced the concept of multiple, partial loan disbursements designed to track the farmers' investment needs, according to the agricultural investment schedules (e.g. sowing, fertilizer application, harvesting). These partial disbursements aimed at circumventing loan diversion as well as reducing the risk of a total loan default.

To mitigate the higher risks associated with the adaptation of loan features, agricultural finance for smallholder farmers requires intensified loan assessment (choosing the right farmers) and loan monitoring. To some extent, choosing the right farmers can even partially mitigate the external risks inherent in agricultural finance, as these farmers are able to harvest the best yields in the face of unfavourable weather conditions and are best positioned to make a profit in the face of market price drops. In contrast to traditional microfinance, loan officers are required to spend more time in the field (or in this case "on the field"). Via physical visits, loan officers collect information on farmers' agricultural performance that would otherwise be difficult to obtain. Loan officers' sound agricultural knowledge is a vital precondition for successful loan assessment and monitoring. In the assessment phase, loan officers are able to use their agricultural knowledge to verify whether or not smallholders are committed, commercially minded, and applying good agricultural techniques. While loan monitoring is partially done by the group, loan officers have to visit smallholder in advance of each new loan disbursement (in most cases at least three times for any given loan). These monitoring visits also enable loan officers to check whether or not there are any signs of a potential risk (e.g. incidences of pests, possible upcoming weather events such as risk of a drought) and correspondingly advice farmers.

Such intensified assessment and monitoring procedures imply high additional costs, especially in remote rural areas. These costs could be partly offset by meeting smallholder farmers in groups, thus seeing 30 at a time instead of individually. Additionally, MFIs aim to keep successful farmers as clients, as each new loan assessment would be less costly. Furthermore, most MFIs collaborate with different stakeholders to reduce their costs. Whenever possible, MFIs work together with existing extension services and the MoA, for example, to help gather information and link farmers to NGOs offering agricultural support services. Technical innovations such as banking through mobile phones, mobile bank branches, or agency banking can also greatly help to reduce costs for MFIs as well as for smallholders, where available.

In addition to the above risk and cost mitigation factors, agricultural finance for smallholder farmers benefits from an additional risk and cost mitigator vis-à-vis traditional microfinance, namely farmers' integration in agricultural value chains. In contrast to financial institutions, which traditionally focus on the direct recipient of a loan and his/her economic activities and securities, lenders to smallholder farmers have the advantage of being able to view the entire agricultural value chain. Doing so helps MFIs to better understand the risks of the particular agricultural product (and thus the farmer) and see potential opportunities to reduce costs and risks. Having the bank pay an input provider directly could, for example, mitigate the risk of loan diversion; collaborating with extension services reduces the costs for monitoring; and cooperating with buyers enables the MFIs to receive farmers' revenues directly to the MFI's account and deduct the loan repayment immediately.

In summary, this paper has endeavoured to demonstrate that smallholder farmers in rural areas can be served by MFIs, who adapt their loan features and lending techniques. The extent of the adaptations is reason enough not to commit to such an endeavour lightly. A strong commitment combined with a well-thought-out business strategy and market analysis is needed to develop appropriate loan products and conduct successful loan assessment and monitoring. Whether such an endeavour can be profitable enough to be sustainable, that is, also attract private non-donor capital (as in the case of traditional microfinance) is outside the scope of this paper. Of the MFIs interviewed for this paper, some have reported being profitable as an agricultural finance player; others have reported difficulties; and still others have expressed hope of reaching profitability within their agricultural lending unit soon. Further investigation is needed to see whether or not the measures described in this paper are cost-effective enough to be viable and to indicate where adaptations can be made to further reduce transaction costs without simultaneously increasing credit risks.

There are committed and innovative players that see beyond the risks, because:

Conclusion

> "You don't do agricultural lending when you're risk adverse. (...) when you look at the sector, the first thing you see is risk. (...) But you must see beyond the risks, because the risks can be mitigated. And everybody is working towards how to mitigate those risks."[155]

MFIs from various institutional backgrounds and countries, stakeholders of agricultural value chains, as well as numerous development partners are keen to address these challenges and make agricultural finance for smallholder farmers' work.

---

[155] Agribusiness General Manager, Equity Bank.

Bibliography

ADAF (Appropriate Development for Africa Foundation) (2013a): Le modèle MC².
http://www.adaf-amc2.org/, visited on August 31, 2013.
ADAF (Appropriate Development for Africa Foundation) (2013b): Rapport financier, exercise 2012, mimeo.
Adams, Dale W./von Pitschke, J.D. (1992): Microenterprise Credit Programs: Déja Vu, in: World Development 20(10), pp. 1463–1470.
Adesina, Akinwumi A. (2010): Conditioning Trends Shaping the Agricultural and Rural Landscape in Africa, in: Agricultural Economics 41(11), pp. 73–82.
AU (African Union/MFW4A (Making Finance Work for Africa) (2011): Zipping Finance and Farming in Africa – Harnessing the Continent's Potential, paper prepared for the Making Finance Work for Africa Conference 29 and 30 June 2011, Kampala: Munyonyo Conference Centre.
Agaru SACCO (2013): Audited financial statements for the year ended 31st December 2012, mimeo.
Agaru SACCO (2010): Agaru SACCO Ltd. Annual Report 2010, Kalongo.
AgriFin (Agricultural Finance Support Facility) (2013): Webinar: Credit scoring for agriculture lending.
http://www.agrifinfacility.org/event/webinar-credit-scoring-agriculture-lending, visited on August 31, 2013.
Andrews, Meagan/MEDA (Mennonite Economic Development Associates) (2006): Microcredit and Agriculture: How to Make it Work, paper presented at the Global Microcredit Summit.
http://www.microcreditsummit.org/papers/Workshops/22_Andrews.pdf, visited on September 25, 2012.
Armendáriz, Bestriz/Morduch, Jonathan (2010): *The Economics of Microfinance*, second edition, Cambridge, London: MIT Press.
Arunachalam, Ramesh S. (2006): What is Portfolio Yield? How to Use It in Microfinance?, in: Sa-Dhan Microfinance Manager Series, Technical Note No. 16.
http://www.sa-dhan.net/Adls/Technicalnotes/Technical_Notes_16.pdf, visited on August 24, 2013.
Beck, Thorsten/Maimbo, Samuel Munzele/Faye, Issa/Triki, Thouraya (2011): *Financing Africa. Through the Crisis and Beyond*, Washington, DC: The World Bank.
Birner, R./Resnick, D (2010): The Political Economy of Policies for Smallholder Agriculture, in: World Development 38(10), pp. 1442–1452.
Binswanger, Hans/Khandker, Shahidur (1995): The Impact of Formal Finance on the Rural Economy in India, in: Journal of Development Studies 32(2) (December), pp. 234–262.
Brandt, Hartmut (2004): *Probleme und Tendenzen der Agrarpolitiken in Subsahara-Afrika*, Bonn: German Development Institute (DIE).
Braun, J. von (2004): Small-Scale Farmers in Liberalised Trade Environment, paper prepared for the seminar on small-scale farmers in liberalized trade environments, 18–19 October 2004, Haikko, Finland.
http://www.helsinki.fi/taloustiede/Abs/Pub38.pdf, visited on August 31, 2013.

Bibliography

Brüntrup, Michael (2008): Instrumente zur Förderung der ländlichen Entwicklung. Bessere Erfolgsaussichten bei Hunger- und Armutsbekämpfung durch Optimierung spezifischer Themenfelder der landwirtschaftlichen Entwicklung, schriftliche Einlassung zur öffentlichen Anhörung des Ausschusses für wirtschaftliche Zusammenarbeit, Bonn: German Development Institute (DIE).

Brüntrup, Michael (2011): Produktivität und Wettbewerbsfähigkeit von Kleinbauern, presentation at the Kleinbauern-AG, October 26, 2011, Bonn: German Development Institute (DIE), mimeo.

BMZ (Bundesministerium für wirtschaftliche Zusammenarbeit und Entwicklung) (2005): Mikrofinanzierung: Entwicklungspolitische Zielsetzung und Subventionsbedarf, Bonn.

Carroll, Tom/Stern, Andrew/Zook, Dan/Funes, Rocio/Rastegar, Angela/Lien, Yuting (2012): Catalyzing Smallholder Agricultural Finance, Dalberg Global Development Advisors.

CGAP (Consultative Group to Assist the Poor) (2013): What is Microfinance?
http://www.cgap.org/about/faq, visited on August 07, 2013.

Chamberlin, Jordan (2007): Defining smallholder agriculture in Ghana: Who are smallholders, what do they do and how are they linked with markets? Ghana Strategy Support Program (GSSP) Background Paper No. 6, Accra: International Food Policy Research Institute (IFPRI).

Charitonenko, Stephanie/Campion, Anita (2003): Expanding Commercial Microfinance in Rural Areas: Constraints and Opportunities. Case Study in the Area of Rural Finance Expansion: Experience in Commercialization at the Paving the Way Forward to Rural Finance Conference.
http://www.microfinancegateway.org/gm/document1.9.26304/19863_19863.pdf, visited on November 3, 2012.

Churchill, Craig/Coster, Dan (2001): Microfinance Risk Management Handbook, CARE.
http://kb.trilincanalytics.com/upload/f5/f546502afcea3e5.pdf, visited on December 8, 2012.

Christen, Robert P./Pearce, Douglas (2005): Managing Risk and Designing Products for Agricultural Microfinance: Features of an Emerging Model, Occasional Paper No. 11, Consultative Group to Assist the Poor (CGAP), International Fund for Agricultural Development (IFAD).
http://www.ifad.org/ruralfinance/pub/risks.pdf, visited on August 31, 2013.

Coetzee, Gerhard/Kabbucho, Kamau/Mnjama, Andrew (2002): Understanding the Re-birth of Equity Building Society in Kenya, Nairobi: MicroSave.
http://www.microfinancegateway.org/gm/document-1.9.27653/3534_st_ebs_rebirth.pdf, visited on May 10, 2013.

COMPACI (Competitive African Cotton Initiative) (2013): Background.
www.compaci.org, visited on September 03, 2013.

CRDB (Centenary Rural Development Bank) (2013a): About Centenary Bank.
http://www.centenarybank.co.ug/content/about-centenary-bank, visited on May 10, 2013.

CRDB (Centenary Rural Development Bank) (2013b): Centelease.
http://www.centenarybank.co.ug/product/business-loans-leases/centelease, visited on September 05, 2013.

CRDB (Centenary Rural Development Bank) (2013c): *Annual Report 2012.*
http://www.centenarybank.co.ug/sites/default/files/reports/annual%20report%202012%20final%20pdf.pdf, visited on June 30, 2013.

Daley-Harris, Sam (2009): State of the Microcredit Summit Campaign Report 2009, Washington: Microcredit Summit.

Dixon, J./Tanyeri-Abur, A./Wattenbach, H. (2004): Framework for analysing impacts of globalization on smallholders, in: Dixon, J./Taniguchi, K./Wattenbach, H./Tanyeri-Arbur, A. (eds.): *Smallholders, Globalization and Policy Analysis, Agricultural Management, Marketing and Finance Service* (AGSF) Occasional Paper No. 5. Rome: FAO.
http://www.fao.org/docrep/007/y5784e/y5784e02.htm, visited on Augsut 31, 2013.

Doran, Alan/McFadyen, Ntongi/Vogel, Robert C. (2009): The Missing Middle in Agricultural Finance. Relieving the Capital Constraint on Smallholder Groups and Other Aricultural SMEs, Oxfam.

Dorward, Andrew R./Kirsten, Johann F./Omamo, S. Were/Poulton, Colin/Vink, Nick (2009): Institutions and the Agricultural Development Challenge in Africa, in: Kirsten, J. F./Dorward, A. R./Poulton, C./Vink, N. (eds.): *Institutional Economics Perspectives on African Agricultural Development*, Washington, DC: International Food Policy Research Institute (IFPRI).

Equity Bank (2013a): Corporate Philosophies.
http://www.equitybank.co.ke/index.php/about/corporate-philosophies, visited on September 02, 2013.

Equity Bank (2013b): Agricultural Loans.
http://www.equitybank.co.ke/index.php/loans/agriculture-loans visited on September 02, 2013.

Equity Bank (2013c): M-Kesho.
http://www.equitybank.co.ke/index.php/self-service/mobile-banking/m-kesho, visited on September 02, 2013.

Equity Bank (2012): Annual Report and Financial Statements 2011, Nairobi.
http://equitybankgroup.com/index.php/investor-relations/financial-results, visited on September 02, 2013.

Equity Bank (2011): Annual Report and Financial Statements 2010, Nairobi.
http://equitybankgroup.com/index.php/investor-relations/financial-results, visited on September 02, 2013.

Faulu (2013a): About Faulu.
http://www.faulukenya.com/index.php?option=com_content&view=article&id=47&Itemid=53, visited on September 05, 2013.

Faulu (2013b): Audited Financial Statements as at 31st December 2012.
http://www.faulukenya.com/index.php?option=com_docman&task=cat_view&gid=66&limit=5&limitstart=0&order=hits&dir=DESC&Itemid=156, visited on June 30, 2013.

FECECAM (Faîtière des Caisses d'Epargne et de Crédit Agricole Mutuel) (2013): Financial Statement 2012.
http://www.mixmarket.org/mfi/fececam/files, visited on June 30, 2013.

FinMark Trust (2011): The status of agricultural and rural financial services in Southern Africa 2011, South Africa.

Gangrade, K. D./Chaturvedi, H. R. (1989): Green Revolution and the Drift in Rural Development, in: Sharma, M. L./Dak, T. M. (eds.): *Green Revolution and Social Change*, Delhi: Ajanta Publications.

138 Bibliography

Gisbert, Lena (2008): Magic Microfinance – bald auch eine Erfolgsgeschichte für Afrika?, GIGA Focus No. 9, Hamburg: GIGA.

Gläser, Jochen/Laudel, Grit (2009): Experteninterviews und qualitative Inhaltsanalyse: Qualitative Inhaltsanalyse, 3. Überarbeitete Version, Wiesbaden: VS Verlag für Sozialwissenschaften.

Goldberg, Mike/Palladini, Eric (2010): Managing risk and creating value with microfinance, Washington, D.C.: World Bank.

Goodland, Andrew/Onumah, Gideon/Amadi, Juliana/Griffith, Geoffrey (1999): *Rural Finance, Policy Series 1*, Chatham: Natural Resource Institute.

Haggblade, S./Hazell, P.B.R./Gabre-Madhin, E. (2010): Challenges for African agriculture, in: Haggblade, S./Hazell, P. B. R. (eds): *Successes in African Agriculture: Lessons for the Future*, Baltimore, MD: Published for the International Food Policy Research Institute (IFPRI) by Johns Hopkins University Press.

Harper, Malcom (2005): Farm credit and micro-finance – Is there a critical mismatch?
http://www.r,> visited on August 23, 2013.

Harper, Malcom (2008): Microfinance and farmers: Do they fit? in: Dichter, T./Harper, M. (eds.): *What's Wrong with Microfinance?*, Rugby, Warwickshire: Practical Action Publishing, pp 83–94.

IAASTD (International Assessment of Agricultural Knowledge, Science and Technology for Development) (2009a): Sub-Saharan Africa (SSA) Report, Washington, DC.
http://www.agassessment.org/, visited on August 02, 2013.

IAASTD (International Assessment of Agricultural Knowledge, Science and Technology for Development) (2009b): Summary for Decisions Makers of the Sub-Saharan Africa (SSA) Report, Washington, DC.
http://www.agassessment.org/, visited on August 02, 2013.

IBLF (International Business Leaders Forum) (2013): Enterprise Development Case Studies. Equity Bank Kilimo Biashara.
http://www.iblf.org/reports-2012/reports-archive/casestudies/EnterpriseCaseStudies.aspx, visited on May 21, 2013.

ICAC (International Cotton Advisory Committee) (2013): Cotton sector reform in CFA Zones, Attachement II to SC-N-524, 5 June 2013, Washington, DC.
https://www.icac.org/getattachment/mtgs/Committee/SC-524/Details/524-Att-2-Cotton-reform-in-CFA.pdf, visited on September 01, 2013.

IFAD (International Fund for Agricultural Development) (2003): Agricultural Marketing Companies as Sources of Smallholder Credit in Eastern and Southern Africa. Experiences, Insights and Potential Donor Role.
http://www.ifad.org/ruralfinance/policy/pf.pdf, visited on August 31, 2013.

IFAD (International Fund for Agricultural Development) /UNEP (United Nations Environment Programme) (2013): Smallholders, Food Security and the Environment.
http://www.ifad.org/climate/resources/smallholders_report.pdf, visited on August 08, 2013.

Iturrioz, Ramiro (2009): *Agricultural Insurance*, Washington, DC: World Bank.
http://siteresources.worldbank.org/FINANCIALSECTOR/Resources/Primer12_Agricultural_Insurance.pdf, visited on August 31, 2013.

Jayne, T.S./Mather, David/Mghenyi, Elliot (2010): Principal Challenges Confronting Smallholder Agriculture in Sub-Saharan Africa, in: World Development 38(10), pp. 1384–1398.

Jessop, Reuben/Diallo, Boubacar/Duursma, Marjan/Mallek, Abdallah/Harms, Job/Manen van, Bert (2012): Creating Access to Agricultural Finance. Based on a horizontal study of Cambodia, Mali, Senegal, Tanzania, Thailand and Tunisia, in: A savoir No 14, Agence Francaise de Développement (AFD).

Johnson, Susan/Malkamaki, Markku/Wanjau, Kuria (2005): Tackling the 'Frontiers' of Microfinance in Kenya: The Role for Decentralized Services, Nairobi: Microsave.

Juhudi Kilimo (2013a): Who we are.
http://www.juhudikilimo.com/juhudi.php?id=3, visited on September 05, 2013.

Juhudi Kilimo (2013b): Why we're different.
http://www.juhudikilimo.com/juhudi.php?id=8, visited on September 05, 2013.

Juhudi Kilimo (2013c): Juhudi Kilimo Company Limited annual report and financial statements 31 December 2012.
http://www.mixmarket.org/sites/default/files/juhudi_kilimo_afs_12.pdf, visited on June 30, 2013.

Kachwanya (2010): The launch of M-Kesho marks the beginning of the end of ATMs.
http://www.kachwanya.com/the-launch-of-m-kesho-marks-the-beginning-of-the-end-of-atms/, visited on September 02, 2013.

Karim, Bazlul M. (1986): *The Green Revolution: An International Bibliography*, New York i.a.: Greenwood Press.

KDA (K-Rep development Agency) (2013): About us.
http://www.k-rep.co.ke/?page_id=28, visited on June 30, 2013.

Kherallah, Mylène/Delgado, Christopher/Gabre-Madhin, Eleni/Minot, Nicholas/Johnson, Michael (2000): The Road Half Traveled: Agricultural Market Reform in Sub-Saharan Africa, Food Policy Report, Washington, DC: IFPRI.
http://www.ifpri.org/publication/road-half-traveled, visited on August 31, 2013.

Kibaara, Betty (2006): Rural Financial Services in Kenya: What is working and why? Tegemeo Institute of Agricultural Policy and Development, Working Paper No. 20/2006, Nairobi.

Klein, Brigitte/Meyer, Richard/Hannig, Alfred/Burnett, Jill/Fiebig, Michael (1999): Better Practices in Agricultural Lending, Agricultural Finance Revisited No. 3, Rome: Food and Agriculture Organization (FAO), Gesellschaft für technische Zusammenarbeit (GTZ).
http://www.fao.org/ag/ags/ags-division/publications/publication/en/c/47555/, visited on June 15, 2013.

Klerk, Mike de/Machethe, Charles/Coetzee, Gerhard (2011): *The Status of Agricultural and Rural Financial Services in Southern Africa 2011*, South Africa: FinMark Trust.

Kyanika NsibaMBFI, Abdul (2010): Centenary Bank's agriculture lending: The Story, in: Roberts, R./Ocaya, R. (eds.): *Agricultural Finance Yearbook 2010. Marrying Finance and Farming.* Kampala: Bank of Uganda, GIZ Financial System Development Programme.

Ledgerwood, Joanna (1999): *Microfinance Handbook. An Institutional and Financial Perspective*, Washington, DC: World Bank.

MFW4A (Making Finance Work for Africa) (2012): Agricultural and Rural Finance.
http://www.mfw4a.org/agricultural-rural-finance/agricultural-rural-finance.html, visited on September 25, 2012.

Matovu, William (2009). Dairy investments by smallholders, in: Roberts, R./Ocaya, R. (eds.): *Agricultural Finance Yearbook 2009. Investment-led Productivity Building in Agricultural Value Chains*, Uganda: Bank of Uganda, GTZ Financial Services Development Programme, pp 98–107.

Mees, Marc/Bombda, Justin (2006): The link between a micro finance institution and the modern banking sector: the case of MC2, the NGO ADAF and Afriland First Bank in Cameroon, Zoom microfinance No. 19/2006, SOS Faim.

Meyer, Richard L. (2009) : Les Services de Microfinance pour l'Agriculture: Potentialités et Défis, in: Morvant-Roux, S. (ed.) : Exclusion et Liens Financiers. Microfinance pour l'agriculture des pays du sud, Rapport 2008–2009, Paris: Economica, pp. 53–66.

Meyer, Richard L. (2011): *Subsidies as an Instrument in Agricultural Finance: A Review*, Washington, DC: The World Bank.

MicroFinance Transparency (2012): Calculating Transparent Pricing Tool – v2.2.
http://www.mftransparency.org/resources/calculating-transparent-pricing-tool/, visited on August 28, 2013.

MicroFinance Transparency (2013a): Centenary Rural Development Bank.
http://www.mftransparency.org/microfinance-pricing/Uganda/mfi/003-V02-Centenary+Bank-20130124/, visited on August 28, 2013.

MicroFinance Transparency (2013b): Juhudi Kilimo Limited Liability Company.
http://data.mftransparency.org/data/institutions/183/?calculationType=&currencyType=74, visited on August 27, 2013.

MicroFinance Transparency (2013c): The Pricing Transparency Index.
http://www.mftransparency.org/wp-content/uploads/2013/03/MFT-BRF-207-EN-The-Pricing-Transparency-Index-2013-03.pdf,> visited on August 31, 2013.

Miller, Calcin/Jones Linda (2010): *Agricultural Value Chain Finance. Tools and Lessons*, Warwickshire, Rome: Food and Agricultural Organization (FAO), Practical Action Publishing.

Ministry of Finance/CRDB (Centenary Rural Development Bank of Uganda) (2002): Financing of Agriculture in the Context of Liberalization, paper presented at Dakar, Senegal, 21–24 January 2002.
http://afm.cirad.fr/documents/4_Services/microfinance/EN/1_Com1.pdf, visited on May 10, 2013.

Mixmarket (2013): Cross-Market Analysis.
http://www.mixmarket.org/profiles-reports/crossmarket-analysis-report, visited on June 30, 2013.

Mixmarket (2014): About MIX.
http://www.mixmarket.org/about, visited November 1, 2014

Morris, Kelly J. (1995): The effects of using credit unions as onlending agents for external lines of credit: The experience of the International Credit Union Movement, Working Paper No. 14, Geneva: International Labour Office.

Morvant-Roux, Solène (2008): What Can Microfinance Contribute to Agriculture in Developing Countries? Proceedings from the International Conference in Paris 4–6 December 2007, Paris: FARM.
http://www.fondation-farm.org/IMG/pdf/Farm_microfinance_conf_eng.pdf, visited on August 31, 2013.

Morvant-Roux, Solène (2009): Financing Agriculture in Developing Countries: Governance Models Promoting Sustainability, in: de Bettignies, H.-C. /Lépineux, F. (eds.): *Finance for a Better World: The Shift Toward Sustainability*, Houndmills, Basingstoke, Hampshire: Palgrave Macmillan, pp. 189–203.

Nagarajan, Geetha/Meyer, Richard L. (2005): Rural Finance: Recent Advances and Emerging Lessons, Debates, and Opportunities, Reformatted Version of Working Paper AEDE-WP-0041-05, Ohio: Department of Agricultural, Environmental, and Development Economics, Ohio State University.

Opio Ogal, Moses (2009): Agaru SACCO: A beacon for tier 4 institutions, in: Roberts, R./Ocaya, R. (eds.): Agricultural Finance Yearbook 2009. Investment-led Productivity Building in Agricultural Value Chains, Bank of Uganda, GTZ Financial Services Development Programme.
http://www.agrifinfacility.org/sites/agrifinfacility.org/files/Agricultural%20Finance%20Yearbook%202009%20-%20Uganda%20-%20GTZ%20etc_0.pdf, visited on August 31, 2013.

Paddock, William/Paddock, Paul (1967): *Famine 1975! America's Decision: Who Will Survive?*, Boston: Little Brown.

Pearce, Douglas (2003): Financial Services for the Rural Poor, CGAP Donor Brief No. 15, Washington, DC: CGAP.
http://www.cgap.org/sites/default/files/CGAP-Donor-Brief-Financial-Services-for-the-Rural-Poor-Oct-2003.pdf, visited on August 08, 2013.

Pearce, Douglas/Reinsch, Myka (2006): Equity Building Society of Kenya reaches rural markets, in: CGAP (Consultative Group to Assist the Poor)/IFAD (International Fund for Agricultural Development) (eds.): Emerging Lessons in Agricultural Microfinance. Selected case studies.
http://www.ifad.org/ruralfinance/pub/case_studies.pdf, visited on July 31, 2013.

Peltzer, Roger/Röttger, Daniela (2013): Cotton Sector Organisation Models and their Impact on Farmer's Productivity and Income, DIE Discussion Paper 4/2013, Bonn: German Development Institute (DIE).

Röttger, Daniela (2012): Die Finanzierung landwirtschaftlicher Werstschöpfungsketten: Herausforerdungen und Lösungsansätze in Sub-Sahara Afrika, in: Theuvsen, L./Voss, A. (eds.): *International High-Value Chains*, Internationale Reihe Agribusiness, Band 11, Göttingen: Cuvillier Verlag, pp. 45–87.

Safaricom (2013). M-Pesa.
http://www.safaricom.co.ke/personal/m-pesa/m-pesa-agents, visited on September 02, 2013.

Seibel, Hans Dieter (2003): Centenary Rural Development Bank, Uganda. A flagship of rural bank reform, in: Africa, Small Enterprise Development 14 (3), pp 35–46.

Sina, James (2012): Index-based weather insurance - International and Kenyan experiences, Adaption to Climate Change and Insurance (ACCI), Deutsche Gesellschaft für Internationale Zusammenarbeit (GIZ), Ministry of Agriculture (MoA).
http://www.acci.co.ke/accio/wp/wp-content/uploads/2013/04/ACCI_Insurance-Experiences_5-12.pdf, visited on July 17, 2013.

Temu, Andrew E. (2009): Innovations in Addressing Rural Finance Challenges in Africa, AFRACA Rural Finance Series No. 6, Nairobi: African Rural and Agricultural Credit Association (AFRACA).
http://www.afraca.org/publications/210AFRACA%20RFS%202009%20Publication%20Draft%2002032009.pdf, visited on November 11, 2012.

UGP/ADAF (Appropriate Development for Africa Foundation) (s.a.) : Procédure de gestion des subventions PPTE dans les Mc2/Muffa, mimeo.

Wehnert, Branko/ Heine, Eckhard (2010): Appraisal report on the development intervention Agaru SACCO. Towards the promotion of agricultural and rural cooperative financial services in the Acholi-Region, German Development Service Uganda, mimeo.

Westercamp, Christine (1999): Federation of the Agricultural Savings and Credit Unions (FECECAM), Benin (Case Study), Eschborn: CGAP Working Group on Savings Mobilization, Deutsche Gesellschaft für technische Zusammenarbeit (GTZ), Bundesministerium für wirtschaftliche Zusammenarbeit und Entwicklung (BMZ).

Wolz, Axel (2005): *The Role of Agriculture and Rural Development in Achieving the Millennium Development Goals - A Joint Donor Narrative*, Bonn: Global Donor Platform for Rural Development (GDPRD).

World Bank (2006): Module 8: Investments in Rural Finance for Agriculture. In: World Bank, Agriculture Investment Sourcebook.
http://go.worldbank.org/CCC68JMIZ0, visited on August 30, 2013.

World Bank (2003): Project Performance Assessment Report, Republic of Benin. Agricultural services restructuring project (Credit 22850, TF 21619), Community-based food security project (Credit 26010, TF 26605), Second rural savings and loans cooperatives rehabilitation project (Credit 25290), Report No. 26207.

Wormgoor, Otto/Ssenyimba, Samuel (2007): Planet Rating: Agaru SACCO, Uganda, Kampala: Planet Rating.
http://www.planetrating.com/generer-pdf/PR_Agaru_2007.pdf-229.htm, visited on August 31, 2013.

Yaron, Jacob/Benjamin, Mc Donald (1997): Developing rural financial markets, in: Finance & Development 34(4), pp. 40–43.
http://www.imf.org/external/pubs/ft/fandd/1997/12/index.htm, visited on April 12, 2011.

Yaron, Jacob/Benjamin, Mc Donald/Piprek, Gerda I. (1997): Rural finance. Issues, designs, and best practice, in: Environmental and socially sustainable development studies and monographs series No. 14, Washington, DC: World Bank.

Yaron, Jacob/Benjamin, Mc Donald (2002): Recent developments in rural finance markets, in: Zeller, M./Meyer, R. L. (eds.): *The Triangle of Microfinance. Financial Sustainability, Outreach, and Impact*, Baltimore: Johns Hopkins University Press, pp. 321–340.

Yumkella, Kandeh K./Patrick M. Kormawa/Torben M. Roepstorff/Anthony M. Hawkins (eds.) (2011): *Agribusiness for Africa's Prosperity*, Vienna: United Nations Industrial Development Organization (UNIDO).

Zeller, Manfred (2003): Models of Rural Financial Institutions, Lead Theme Paper at the Conference Paving the Way Forward for Rural Finance.
http://www.microfinancegateway.org/p/site/m/template.rc/1.9.27515/, visited on April 12, 2011.

Annex

Annex A: Interview partner

No.	Position of interview partner	Institution	Country
Commercial banks			
01	Agribusiness General Manager	Equity Bank	Kenya
02	(1) Credit Officer for Agriculture (2) Relationship Officer for Agriculture	Equity Bank; Kikuyu branch	Kenya
03	Loan Officer for Agriculture	CRDB, Lira branch	Uganda
Microfinance companies			
04	Agribusiness Development Manager	Faulu	Kenya
05	Agricultural Product Specialist	RUCREF	Uganda
06	Consultant for Performance Management	Juhudi Kilimo	Kenya
Membership-based financial institutions			
07	Loan Officer for Agriculture	Agaru SACCO, Kalongo branch	Uganda
08	(1) Branch manager (2) Manager Loans and Agricultural System Administrator	(1) Agaru SACCO, Pader branch (2) Agaru SACCO; Head Office	Uganda
09	General Manager	CLCAM Kouandé	Benin
10	General Manager	CLCAM Pehunco	Benin
11	Executive Secretary	ADAF	Cameroon
12	Head of Accounting and Control of MicroBank Department	ADAF	Cameroon
13	Accountant	ADAF	Cameroon
Consultants			
14	Consultant for Microfinance and Value Chain Finance	COMPACI	Benin
15	Financial Development Consultant	aBi Trust	Uganda
16	Agricultural Insurance Expert	Jubilee Insurance	Kenya
17	Executive Manager	Uganda Coffee Farmer Alliance (UCFA)	Uganda
18	General Manager East Africa	Neumann Foundation	Uganda

Annex B: Median yield on gross portfolio (real)

Table I: Median yield on gross portfolio (real) of MFIs worldwide

Sustainability	Fiscal year	MFIs (count)	Yield on gross portfolio (real) (median)
Non-OSS	2009	394	20.07%
Non-OSS	2010	341	21.14%
Non-OSS	2011	303	19.64%
OSS	2009	853	17.90%
OSS	2010	976	21.85%
OSS	2011	934	17.34%

Source: calculated with Mixmarket (2013).

Table II: Median yield on gross portfolio (real) of self-sustainable MFIs in different world regions

Region	Fiscal year	MFIs (count)	Yield on gross portfolio (real) (median)
Africa	2009	355	22.79%
Africa	2010	337	25.84%
Africa	2011	325	22.41%
East Asia and the Pacific	2009	191	26.04%
East Asia and the Pacific	2010	192	19.64%
East Asia and the Pacific	2011	229	17.83%
Eastern Europe and Central Asia	2009	270	20.94%
Eastern Europe and Central Asia	2010	253	22.03%
Eastern Europe and Central Asia	2011	227	18.55%
Latin America and The Caribbean	2009	408	27.11%
Latin America and The Caribbean	2010	425	25.91%
Latin America and The Caribbean	2011	407	25.27%
Middle East and North Africa	2009	73	25.29%
Middle East and North Africa	2010	71	21.36%
Middle East and North Africa	2011	59	19.09%
South Asia	2009	259	15.50%
South Asia	2010	257	12.88%
South Asia	2011	228	12.14%

Source: calculated with Mixmarket (2013).

Table III: Median yield on gross portfolio (real) for African MFIs

Sustainability	Fiscal year	MFIs (count)	Yield on gross portfolio (real) (median)
Non-OSS	2009	113	23.93%
Non-OSS	2010	98	23.43%
Non-OSS	2011	86	22.23%
OSS	2009	110	21.08%
OSS	2010	130	26.11%
OSS	2011	127	21.89%

Source: calculated with Mixmarket (2013).

Table IV: Median yield on gross portfolio for African MFIs of different sizes

Scale	Fiscal year	MFIs (count)	Yield on gross portfolio (real) (median)
Large	2009	66	19.49%
Large	2010	64	24.29%
Large	2011	72	21.40%
Medium	2009	86	19.24%
Medium	2010	80	23.33%
Medium	2011	84	20.55%
Small	2009	191	27.95%
Small	2010	177	26.11%
Small	2011	159	26.91%

Source: calculated with Mixmarket (2013).

Annex C: Agricultural loans—calculation of EIRs

Table 1: Short-term loans—effective vs. quoted interest rate

The EIR was calculated for a 6-month and a 12-month loan, with interest rates paid monthly and principle at the end of the loan term in one lump sum, thus it makes no difference whether it is calculated on flat or declining method.

	CB			MFC			MBFI		
	Equity Bank		CRDB	Faulu	Juhudi Kilimo	Agaru SACCO	CLCAM (Pehunco, Kouande)		MC[a]
Loan	Farm input Loan	Grain & hortic. small scale	Micro-enterprises	Agric. loan	Loan for cereal farmers	Asset finance loans	Agric. loan	Agric. loan	COM-PACI loan	Agric. loan (PAD)
Quoted i (% p.a.)	15	10	15	46[1]	20	32[2]	18	24	12	≤12[3]
Fees & charges	LACE[4]: 3%	LACE: 3%	LACE: 3%	Application fee: USD 2	Crop insurance: 3%	Application fee: 1%	Administration fee: USD 4	Cash collateral: 20%	Cash collateral: 10%	Application fee: 0.5-1%
	Credit life insurance: 0.325% (ongoing)	Credit life insurance: 0.325%	Credit life insurance: 0.325%	Commitment fee: 2%	Life insurance: 1%	Loan insurance: 1%	Loan protection fund: 2%	Life insurance: USD 3 + 0.075% (ongoing)	Life insurance: USD 3 + 0.075% (ongoing)	Insurance: 0.6%
					Cash collateral: 10%	Cash collateral: 15%	Commitment fee: 2%			Credit releasing fee: 0.6-0.75%
EIR (% p.a.)	24-28	18-21	24-28	63-68	31-37	57-59	28-36	39-41	17-19	16-18
Deviation (%) (i – EIR)	9-13	8-11	9-13	17-22	11-17	25-27	10-18	15-17	5-7	4-6
PTI (%)	61-68	51-59	61-68	87-92	63-73	68-69	58-72	68-72	68-75	71-83

[a] After three loans, interest rate is reduced to 28%; quoted interest rate from Interview, fees and charges are from MicroFinance Transparency (2013a).
[2] Quoted interest rate taken from Interview, fees and charges from MicroFinance Transparency (2013b); calculated on reducing balance, 2 months grace period and equal monthly installments.
[3] Different MC's had different calculate methods for interest rates (flat or reducing) and charge different fees and charges; figures used are based on information from six MC's, figures in bold used taken for calculation. Quoted interest rate of PAD/PPTE loan always have to be 12% or smaller.
[4] Loan Application and Credit Evaluation fee (LACE).

Source: Interviews (2011) and own calculation with MicroFinance Transparency (2012).

Table II: Medium-/long-term loans—effective vs. quoted interest rate

The EIR was calculated for a loan period of 18 months and 24 months for all loans except Agaru SACCOs tractor loan and CRDBs microleasing. The tractor loan was calculated for a loan term of up to 36 months and microleasing for a loan period up to 5 years. Repayment schedules for all agricultural loans were flexible and adapted to the crop cycle. To be able to compare the different products, the EIR was calculated with the following repayment schedule: principle and interest repayment every 6 months. A difference calculation was made for Juhudi Kilimo and CRDB's microleasing, as they both indicated that they have monthly repayments with the possibility of grace periods. Thus, for Juhudi Kilimo, the EIR was calculated using a grace period of 2 months and monthly repayments afterwards (e.g. a typical loan for a cow) and for CRDB's microleasing the EIR was calculated using a grace period of 6 months and monthly repayments afterwards.

	CB				MFC			MBFI		
	Equity Bank			CRDB	Juhudi Kilimo	Agaru SACCO		CLCAM (Pehunco, Kouandé)		MC²
Loan	Agric. commercial	Farm development	Modern agric. equipment	Microleasing	Dairy farming	Animal traction	Tractor finance	Agric. loan	COMPACI agric. loan	Agric. loan (PAD)
Quoted i (% p.a.)	18 (red.)	17 (flat p.a.)	10 (flat p.a.)	18.96 (red.)	32 (red.)	18 (red.)	18 (red.)	24 (red.)	12 (red.)	≤12 (red.)[1]	≤12 (flat)[1]
Fees and charges	LACE: 3%	LACE: 3%	LACE: 3%	Application fee: min. USD 20	Appl. fee: 1%	Admin. fee: USD 4	admin. fee: USD 4	Cash collateral: 12%	Cash collateral: 10%	Application fee: 0.5-1%	Application fee: 0.5-1%
	Credit life insurance: 0.325% (ongoing)	Credit life insurance: 0.325%	Credit life insurance: 0.325% (ongoing)	Risk factor: 1 - 6%(p.a.)	Life insurance: 1%	Loan protection fund: 2%	Loan protection fund: 2%	Life insurance: USD 3 + 0.075% (ongoing)	Life insurance: USD 3 + 0.075% (ongoing)	Insurance: 0.6%	Insurance: 0.6%
					Cow insurance: 4%	Commitment fee: 2%	Commitment fee: 2%			Releasing fee: 0.6-0.75%	Releasing fee: 0.6-0.75%
					Cash collateral: 15%	Cash collateral: USD 80					
EIR (%) p.a.)	22-23	30-31	19	33-36	56-58	36-37	23-25	38	16	15	21-22
Deviation (%) (i – EIR)	4-5	13-14	9	14-17	24-26	18-19	5-7	14	4	3	9-10
PTI (%)	83-85	59-60	54	62-75	62-64	53-54	75-83	68-69	79	82-85	58-59

Around 70% of all MC's have reducing interest rates while the rest has flat interest rates. Thus, both calculations were made.

Source: Interviews (2011) and own calculation with MicroFinance Transparency (2012).

UNIVERSITY MEETS MICROFINANCE

edited by PlaNet Finance Deutschland e.V.

ISSN 2190-2291

1   *Pim Engels*
    Mission Drift in Microfinance
    The Influence of Institutional and Country Risk Indicators on the Trade-Off between the Financial and Social Performance of Microfinance Institutions
    ISBN 978-3-8382-0123-8

2   *Thilo Klein*
    Microfinance 2.0
    Group Formation and Repayment Performance in Online Lending Platforms During the US Credit Crunch
    ISBN 978-3-8382-0118-4

3   *Saikumar C. Bharamappanavara*
    The Performance Of Microcredit Organisations
    A Comparative Perspective
    ISBN 978-3-8382-0121-4

4   *Oliver Rogall*
    Microfinance and Vulnerability to Poverty
    The Evidence from Rural Households in Cambodia
    ISBN 978-3-8382-0237-2

5   *Maria Cristina De Lorenzo*
    Microfinance Investment Funds: An analysis of profitability
    ISBN 978-3-8382-0251-8

6   *Sascha Huijsman*
    The Impact of the Current Economic and Financial Crisis on Microfinance
    ISBN 978-3-8382-0235-8

7   *Funmilayo A. Akinosi, Daniel Nordlund, Alejandro Turbay*
    Sustainable Microfinance
    Redefining the Socio-Economic Mission in Microfinance
    ISBN 978-3-8382-0334-8

8   *Anna Custers*
    Furthering Financial Literacy
    Experimental Evidence from a Financial Literacy Training Programme for Microfinance Clients in Bhopal, India
    ISBN 978-3-8382-0337-9

9   *Thilo Klein*
    Why Do India's Urban Poor Choose to Go Private?
    Health Policy Simulations in Slums of Hyderabad
    ISBN 978-3-8382-0238-9

10 Nicole Tode
    Transforming Microfinance Institutions
    A possible way to go for Moroccan Microcredit Associations
    ISBN 978-3-8382-0494-9

11 Daniela Röttger
    Agricultural Finance for Smallholder Farmers
    Rethinking Traditional Microfinance Risk and Cost Management Approaches
    ISBN 978-3-8382-0745-2

Sie haben die Wahl:
Bestellen Sie die Schriftenreihe
University Meets Microfinance
einzeln oder im **Abonnement**

per E-Mail: vertrieb@ibidem-verlag.de |per Fax (0511/262 2201)
als Brief (*ibidem*-Verlag | Leuschnerstr. 40 | 30457 Hannover)

Bestellformular

☐ Ich abonniere die Schriftenreihe *University Meets Microfinance*
ab Band # _____

☐ Ich bestelle die folgenden Bände der Schriftenreihe
University Meets Microfinance
____; ____; ____; ____; ____; ____; ____; ____; ____; ____

Lieferanschrift:

Vorname, Name ....

Anschrift ....

E-Mail.. | Tel.: ....

Datum .... | Unterschrift ....

Ihre Abonnement-Vorteile im Überblick:
- Sie erhalten jedes Buch der Schriftenreihe pünktlich zum Erscheinungstermin – immer aktuell, ohne weitere Bestellung durch Sie.
- Das Abonnement ist jederzeit kündbar.
- Die Lieferung ist innerhalb Deutschlands versandkostenfrei.
- Bei Nichtgefallen können Sie jedes Buch innerhalb von 14 Tagen an uns zurücksenden.

ibidem-Verlag
Melchiorstr. 15
D-70439 Stuttgart
info@ibidem-verlag.de

www.ibidem-verlag.de
www.ibidem.eu
www.edition-noema.de
www.autorenbetreuung.de